D0706630

Genocide

The Act as Idea

Pennsylvania Studies in Human Rights
Bert B. Lockwood Jr., Series Editor

A complete list of books in the series
is available from the publisher.

Genocide

The Act as Idea

Berel Lang

PENN

UNIVERSITY OF PENNSYLVANIA PRESS

PHILADELPHIA

Copyright © 2017 University of Pennsylvania Press
All rights reserved. Except for brief quotations used for purposes of review
or scholarly citation, none of this book may be reproduced in any form by
any means without written permission from the publisher.

Published by
University of Pennsylvania Press
Philadelphia, Pennsylvania 19104-4112
www.upenn.edu/pennpress

Printed in the United States of America

A Cataloging-in-Publication record is available from the
Library of Congress

Cover design by John Hubbard

ISBN 978-0-8122-4885-2 hardcover
ISBN 978-0-8122-9364-7 e-book

*For Lela, Nina, and Gabriel Kornfeld
and Hannah, Leah, and David Riegel*

Simon Dubnow: "Obviously if killing one man is a crime, killing of entire races and peoples must be an even greater one."

Raphael Lemkin: "Killing an individual is a domestic crime—every nation deals with it . . . But murder of a whole people must be recognized as an international crime, which should concern not just one nation but the entire world."

> —Raphael Lemkin's account of a conversation with Simon Dubnow in Riga, 1940.

[Soon afterward, Lemkin escaped to the United States; Dubnow was killed by the Nazis in December 1941.]

Contents

My book's purpose is a defense of the concept and term "genocide" as it has evolved and been applied to the *act* of genocide that had a much longer history. Admittedly, even claiming a need for such a defense may seem questionable, since the concept is now so familiar and carries such weight in legal, moral, and popular discourse, announced in newspapers as well as learned journals, that a predictable reaction might be to ask why the term or idea would warrant a defense any more than the phenomenon itself would deserve one. But a defense *is* called for, in part because "genocide," from its first appearance and continually since, has been criticized, conceptually and in its applications, on grounds of vagueness, obscurity, inconsistency—in sum, as inadequate for what it professes as its purpose. Such criticism has been accompanied, moreover, by proposals for replacement terms claiming to accomplish whatever "genocide" is intended to, and to manage that without its alleged faults. Beyond this, the concept has been charged with a failure to accomplish the goals ascribed to its formulation in the United Nations' Genocide Convention (to "prevent" and to "punish" genocide) and also with opening itself to misuses of the term, as it has become virtually a catchall synonym for atrocity. If the concept of "genocide" is to sustain the legal and moral weight it has acquired, then this nest of basic and varied objections warrants a response that confronts and assesses them. It is this I attempt here, incorporating proposals based on certain of the charges, yet insisting on what I argue is the very important contribution that "genocide" has made to ethical and legal discourse. Far from conceding that the term should be discarded and replaced, as its most extreme critics have urged, I believe this incorporation strengthens its claims in asserting the distinctive crime of group-murder. The effectiveness of "genocide" itself, in naming, defining, and calling attention to the extreme phenomenon it refers to, is, I hope to show, compelling; the following discussion brings evidence and arguments to support this claim.

The book moves, then, along three related lines: first, analyzing the specific reference of the concept of "genocide" in its recognition of genocide as a distinctive act and crime; second, analyzing a number of objections raised in the pushback against "genocide" in its formulation and practical applications, and (as related to these) assessing the alternative terms or concepts proposed for replacing it; and third, responding with proposals for changes to certain flaws in "genocide" as identified by its critics although, as warranted, also by its advocates. The analysis as a whole revolves around the canonical formulation of "genocide" in the United Nations Convention on the Prevention and Punishment of the Crime of Genocide, which was passed by the General Assembly meeting in Paris on December 9, 1948 and which provides still the authoritative—unamended—definition of the crime. (The text of the Convention appears in the book's first section.) This durability at least suggests the force of the basic concept of "genocide," although the near-certain difficulty

2

of reaching agreement on formal revision of the Convention in the present United Nations (with 193 nation-members now, in contrast to the 56 nation-members at the time of the Convention's initial, unanimous adoption) has clearly been a factor. One has also to recognize—a point to be addressed later—that the same avoidance of revision has found channels for criticism through other conventions or declarations related to human rights (such as the Universal Declaration of Human Rights) that might be taken to include the crime of genocide without specifically mentioning it and thus also accepting the problems found in it. In this sense, the defense here is a response *also* to avoidance or neglect.

Even aside from the assessment of specific points and means of criticism directed at it, the Genocide Convention has had an arguably irreversible impact on public and formal thought and practice. This effect is not itself proof of cogency, but it does suggest that any objections to the Convention and thus to "genocide" will have the burden of providing positive proposals that *also* take account of the specific character of genocide—in this way retaining the core of the Convention. That the *charge* of genocide has also been misused in political, cultural, and popular discourse is indisputable, but the fault in that, it seems clear, has been in the concept's abuse, not in the concept. That the Genocide Convention has not since its adoption "prevented" occurrences of genocide as its title affirms is no more an argument against the Convention than is the violation of any other laws or regulations. The deterrent effect of laws is debatable in this instance as others; in any event, deterrence is not the only purpose or function of such legislation.

Thus the design of my account here and its defense of "genocide": to analyze the principal objections that have challenged "genocide" conceptually and to scrutinize the alternative terms proposed as its replacements, recognizing warranted changes in the normative thinking about genocide. Why does such a defense matter? Most obviously because genocide itself matters: the act of group-murder that until the mid-twentieth century had remained an unidentified form of murder, unspecified in either the law or moral reflection. In the view defended here, the naming and conceptualization of the act of genocide marks a notable advance in the history of moral and legal thought—progress impelled by the need to catch up with the "progress" in human imagination and conduct that produced the acts of genocide themselves.

More than anyone else contributing to this advance in legislative and practical consequences as well as its conceptual formulation, Raphael Lemkin, coiner of the term "genocide," warrants recognition. Such recognition has been slow in coming, and the discussion here, appearing almost simultaneously with several other books attesting to the theoretical and practical importance of his role, joins the effort to rectify that. It should be noted that Lemkin's efforts on behalf of "genocide" also took an arguably decisive step in advancing the concept of group-rights, a still broader political and moral principle. Although Lemkin himself rarely used the term "group-rights," the concept is implicit: to identify genocide as a crime against a group's existence without presupposing a group's "right to life," analogous to a "right to life" for individuals violated by individual murder, would be inconsistent—and this Lemkin recognized in just those words. The efforts required to realize these accomplishments were for Lemkin a lifelong, single-minded, and lonely struggle against traditional preconceptions and established political interests—a struggle epitomized in his early and solitary death. His monument was of his own design: the UN Convention on the Prevention and Punishment of the Crime of Genocide.

***

A number of chapters in the book were written initially for separate occasions as lectures, invited papers, and essay reviews; chapters that were also published in earlier versions have been substantially revised. Citations and background references are included, by chapter, in the section "Bibliographical Notes."

I am indebted to many friends and colleagues who generously contributed readings, hearings, and discussions to the book. They have also at times been generous in their criticism—and since I've not always incorporated what they had to say along those lines, my appreciation necessarily extends with a no-fault clause. So thanks from these several directions to Brian Fay, Simone Gigliotti, Yaakov Golomb, the late Tony Judt, Ethan Kleinberg, Joel Kraemer, Leslie Morris, Howard Needler, Dalia Ofer, Andy Rabinbach, Hayden White, Elhanan Yakira, and Steven Zipperstein. Susan Laity has been an invaluable editor of the manuscript, and I am especially indebted to Peter A. Agree of the University of Pennsylvania Press for his more-than-editorial help. Barbara L. Estrin's direct contributions have been among the many devoted and imaginative ways in which she has sustained the book's— and our—history.

Preface

The book is dedicated to my grandchildren in the hope that in their time they may find the issues the book addresses obsolete.

B. L.

New York, 2016

The United Nations Convention on the
Prevention and Punishment of the
Crime of Genocide

The central historical and still canonical formulation of the concept of genocide remains the Convention on the Prevention and Punishment of the Crime of Genocide passed by the General Assembly of the United Nations, on December 9, 1948 and unamended since then.

✶✶✶✶✶✶✶✶✶✶✶✶✶✶✶✶✶✶✶✶✶✶✶✶✶✶✶✶✶✶✶✶✶✶✶

Article 1

The Contracting Parties confirm that genocide, whether committed in time of peace or in time of war, is a crime under international law which they undertake to prevent and to punish.

Article 2

In the present Convention, genocide means any of the following acts committed with intent to destroy, in whole or in part, a national, ethnical, racial or religious group, as such:

(a) Killing members of the group;
(b) Causing serious bodily or mental harm to members of the group;
(c) Deliberately inflicting on the group conditions of life calculated to bring about its physical destruction in whole or in part;
(d) Imposing measures intended to prevent births within the group;
(e) Forcibly transferring children of the group to another group.

Article 3

The following acts shall be punishable:

(a) Genocide;
(b) Conspiracy to commit genocide;
(c) Direct and public incitement to commit genocide;
(d) Attempt to commit genocide;
(e) Complicity in genocide.

Article 4

Persons committing genocide or any of the other acts enumerated in Article 3 shall be punished, whether they are constitutionally responsible rulers, public officials or private individuals.

Article 5

The Contracting Parties undertake to enact, in accordance with their respective Constitutions, the necessary legislation to give effect to the provisions of the present Convention and, in particular, to provide effective penalties for persons guilty of genocide or any of the other acts enumerated in Article 3.

Article 6

Persons charged with genocide or any of the other acts enumerated in Article 3 shall be tried by a competent tribunal of the State in the territory of which the act was committed, or by such international penal tribunal as may have jurisdiction with respect to those Contracting Parties which shall have accepted its jurisdiction.

Article 7

Genocide and the other acts enumerated in Article 3 shall not be considered as political crimes for the purpose of extradition.

The Contracting Parties pledge themselves in such cases to grant extradition in accordance with their laws and treaties in force.

Article 8

Any Contracting Party may call upon the competent organs of the United Nations to take such action under the Charter of the United Nations as they consider appropriate for the prevention and suppression of acts of genocide or any of the other acts enumerated in Article 3.

Article 9

Disputes between the Contracting Parties relating to the interpretation, application or fulfilment of the present Convention, including those relating to the responsibility of a State for genocide or any of the other acts enumerated in Article 3, shall be submitted to the International Court of Justice at the request of any of the parties to the dispute.

Article 10

The present Convention, of which the Chinese, English, French, Russian and Spanish texts are equally authentic, shall bear the date of 9 December 1948.

Article 11

The present Convention shall be open until 31 December 1949 for signature on behalf of any Member of the United Nations and of any non-member State to which an invitation to sign has been addressed by the General Assembly.

The present Convention shall be ratified, and the instruments of ratification shall be deposited with the Secretary-General of the United Nations.

After 1 January 1950, the present Convention may be acceded to on behalf of any Member of the United Nations and of any non-member State which has received an invitation as aforesaid.

Instruments of accession shall be deposited with the Secretary-General of the United Nations.

Article 12

Any Contracting Party may at any time, by notification addressed to the Secretary-General of the United Nations, extend the application of the present Convention to all or any of the territories for the conduct of whose foreign relations that Contracting Party is responsible.

Article 13

On the day when the first twenty instruments of ratification or accession have been deposited, the Secretary-General shall draw up a procès-verbal and transmit a copy of it to each Member of the United Nations and to each of the non-member States contemplated in Article 11.

The present Convention shall come into force on the ninetieth day following the date of deposit of the twentieth instrument of ratification or accession.

Any ratification or accession effected subsequent to the latter date shall become effective on the ninetieth day following the deposit of the instrument of ratification or accession.

Article 14

The present Convention shall remain in effect for a period of ten years as from the date of its coming into force.

It shall thereafter remain in force for successive periods of five years for such Contracting Parties as have not denounced it at least six months before the expiration of the current period.

Denunciation shall be effected by a written notification addressed to the Secretary-General of the United Nations.

Article 15

If, as a result of denunciations, the number of Parties to the present Convention should become less than sixteen, the Convention shall cease to be in force as from the date on which the last of these denunciations shall become effective.

Article 16

A request for the revision of the present Convention may be made at any time by any Contracting Party by means of a notification in writing addressed to the Secretary-General.

The General Assembly shall decide upon the steps, if any, to be taken in respect of such request.

Article 17

The Secretary-General of the United Nations shall notify all Members of the United Nations and the non-member States contemplated in Article 11 of the following:

(a) Signatures, ratifications and accessions received in accordance with Article 11;
(b) Notifications received in accordance with Article 12;
(c) The date upon which the present Convention comes into force in accordance with Article 13;
(d) Denunciations received in accordance with Article 14;
(e) The abrogation of the Convention in accordance with Article 15;
(f) Notifications received in accordance with Article 16.

Article 18

The original of the present Convention shall be deposited in the archives of the United Nations.

A certified copy of the Convention shall be transmitted to all Members of the United Nations and to the non-member States contemplated in Article 11.

Article 19

The present Convention shall be registered by the Secretary-General of the United Nations on the date of its coming into force.

Notes

Article 1 asserts that "genocide, whether committed in time of peace or in time of war, is a crime under international law." The phrase "in time of peace or in time of war" was intended to protect group-identity within national boundaries when that identity is threatened by the ruling government as an "internal" matter as well as across national boundaries.

Article 2 specifies the types and modalities of actions that qualify as genocidal. One requirement is that for any act to be considered genocide, there must be an "intent" to commit genocide (Article 3 cites this as the "attempt" to commit genocide). This condition is the equivalent of the standard legal phrase of "mens rea," in this instance evidently applying it to corporate decisions or actions in addition to its more usual applications to individual "minds." It also marks a crucial difference between genocide and other charges of murder: in individual homicide, for example, the difference between the intent to kill and the actual killing is essential for distinguishing those two criminal acts. But genocide need not be fully "successful" in order to count as genocide; the intent alone suffices, although obviously certain actions would be required to warrant the finding of intent.

Article 2 also distinguishes the specific groups "eligible" for genocide: "national, ethnical, racial or religious groups." This provision has often been criticized for omitting other important groups (e.g., political or economic) and as including groups whose definitions can be challenged (e.g., as the lines of racial identity have been denied or seen as blurred). But that other groups might be added to the four cited does not nullify the finding of *their* past and continued social significance. A further stipulation of Article 2 is that genocide can be committed by a variety of means of which literal (physical) murder is only one. Other means include "measures intended to prevent births within the group" or "forcibly transferring children of the group to another group." The latter two methods underscore the Convention's design to protect the existence of groups. Group sterilization, for example, would ensure the disappearance of the group after a generation; no murder would have been committed, but the group itself would have been destroyed.

Article 4 stipulates that "persons committing genocide . . . shall be punished whether they are constitutionally responsible rulers, public officials or private individuals." This stipulation is directed mainly against the defense in trials of individuals charged with crimes in contexts where a recognizable chain of command is evident: the "I was only following orders" defense. Article 4 asserts that where genocide is charged, this defense has no force.

Article 9 holds that charges of genocide may, as brought by one of the parties, be heard by an international tribunal. At the time of the Convention's adoption, this would have been the International Court of Justice as an organ of the UN; since 2002, the International Criminal Court, independent of the UN, has been specifically charged as one of its responsibilities with identifying and prosecuting the crime of genocide.

Part I

Between Genocide and "Genocide"

The Evil in Genocide

A title I chose *not* to use for this opening chapter would have been blunter: "What's So Bad about Genocide, Anyway?" That flippant wording asks more forthrightly the question considered here of precisely what is distinctive—so bad or wrong—in the act of genocide. The answer to this is often regarded as self-evident, but it is demonstrably far from that, with the definition of "genocide" often disputed and its alleged referent at times even denied. Furthermore, the assumption that the evil in genocide is obvious has led to both over- and misuse of the term and to distortions in identifying its referent. The question of the evil in genocide—what *is* so bad about it—is the subject here, with my premise that genocide is indeed an evil, distinctive in its working, and among the wrongs humanly imagined and perpetrated as wrongful as any other has been shown to be. Nobody is likely to find this assessment surprising or contentious: it would be difficult to name an act or event commonly regarded as more heinous. Genocide, once it was named and described, has come to occupy a place among the most serious offenses in humanity's lengthy—undoubtedly still growing—list of moral and legal violations. But the precise nature of the wrong that "genocide" designates is often ignored or blurred (if only because it is often taken for granted) or, more seriously, misunderstood.

This view of a combination of acceptance and misunderstanding of the significance of the crime of genocide is supported by two readily accessible items of evidence. First, the charge of genocide has become a metaphor for atrocities in general, some of which, on inspection, are clearly not genocide. Poverty, avertable disease, and slavery (for example) have variously been labeled "genocide" or "genocidal," and although these have indeed at times been instruments of genocide, claims of an *intrinsic* connection between such phenomena and genocide, terrible as each is, are dubious. Human history includes many reprehensible acts and events, but relatively few have been genocidal. Nonetheless, "genocide" as a virtual synonym for atrocity has become the equivalent of a curse, and however strained or misleading this usage may be, its figurative expansion reflects a basis in the term's literal meaning. Figurative expression, after all, is anchored in the world as it is, in literal meaning—and the moral charge attached to "genocide," the murder of a group as a group, provides an immediate source for moral outrage given the universal significance and constancy of group-identity.

The second piece of evidence for the extreme character of genocide stems from the history of the word itself—the fact that a new term had to be coined (recently, in historical terms: 1944) in order to name the crime it denoted, implying also that a new concept had to be *thought*, one that reflected either new circumstances or old circumstances newly pushed to an extreme (arguably an expanding moral consciousness or imagination applied to the phenomenon of evil). To be sure, this recent conceptual development does not mean that genocide had not *occurred* previously. There has indeed been disagreement on its historical appearances, ranging from claims on one side that the Holocaust, the Nazi genocide against the Jews, was unique, a novum, in its genocidal character to claims on the other side (in the majority) that earlier occurrences of genocide, from biblical and classical times forward, had all the requisite features of genocide, however distinctive the scale of the Holocaust would later be.

But there is no disagreement about the novelty of the *term* "genocide" or (by implication) of the concept underlying it. These were shaped largely by the efforts of a single person, the Polish Jewish jurist Raphael Lemkin who, after a number of other attempts in the 1930s at formulating and naming the concept and having it entered into international law, introduced the term essentially as it has now come to be acknowledged in his 1944 book, *Axis Rule in Occupied Europe*. During this period, Lemkin was working his way toward a definition of the new term as a needed legal and moral advance, since in his view no other term or phrase in the legal or moral vocabulary adequately expressed its meaning: not "murder," not "mass murder," not even the catchall but vaguer "crime against humanity." Genocide, the phenomenon of *group-murder* (joining the Greek and Latin roots "genos" and "cide"), was in his view distinct from all of these, distinct as an act and distinct in its moral character, its evil—the latter both for the wrong specific to its occurrences and (as I attempt to show) for its enlargement on the concept of evil as such.

Chapter 1

First, then, to the specific evil of genocide. To represent this connection requires retracing certain steps in the history of "genocide," with a focus on the gap it was meant to fill. Legal and moral thinking, like nature in its classical formula, at once abhors a vacuum and does nothing in vain. When a new concept appears among the layers of wrongdoing, then it is reasonable to assume that it would gain traction only if it fills an absence among extant legal and moral categories. And just such a lack stood behind the formulation of the concept of genocide as a distinctive crime, which Lemkin set out to identify, beginning with his initial effort in the context of an international congress in Madrid in 1933 (where the written document he submitted—he was forbidden by his superiors in Warsaw to attend—spoke not of "genocide" but of "barbarity" [physical destruction] and "vandalism" [cultural destruction]), moving then to fuller articulation in his 1944 book, written by him with enough of the Nazi atrocities already in plain view to intensify the need for understanding. The concept of genocide that emerged from this process was subsequently put to use in the planning for the Nuremberg trials (through the International Military Tribunal) of 1945 and the many trials following them, in both Germany and the countries it had occupied or attacked; it was a tacit factor in many of these, although "genocide" rarely appeared in them as a *formal* prosecutorial charge. This early phase of the new concept's history advanced dramatically soon afterward in the newly founded United Nations, first in a General Assembly resolution in 1946 and then in the 1948 Convention on the Punishment and Prevention of the Crime of Genocide. The history of the concept and its applications continues to unfold, including most notably the activation of the International Criminal Court, ratified by member countries in 2002, for prosecuting the crime of genocide which was specifically named as one of the Court's charges together with "crimes against humanity" and "war crimes." Other tribunals initiated earlier by the International Court of Justice under the auspices of the United Nations (e.g., the international tribunals for the former Yugoslavia and for Rwanda) have also conducted hearings on charges of genocide (among other charges). The tribunal for the former Yugoslavia, for example, handed down 161 indictments for crimes under its jurisdiction; two trials including the charge of genocide are ongoing in the cases of Ratko Mladic and Radovan Karadzik.

Raphael Lemkin's work affected all these stages of thinking and legislation about genocide. The crime he labored to bring to the world's attention seems now so obvious that we might suppose that there were reasons (not necessarily good ones) why it had not been identified earlier, and one such reason seems especially relevant to understanding the concept itself. Modern international law had viewed the nation-state as its basic structural unit; international crimes were, on the standard model, accepted crimes committed by one nation against another or others. The implications of this restriction were straightforward: no country had a recognizable "interest" in another country's treatment of its citizens or of minorities, whether citizens or not, within its own boundaries; so far as concerned that country's individual inhabitants, the obligations even of nations at war were primarily to other nations, with little thought for the enemy nation's noncitizens and none at all for

groups unprotected by citizenship. To be sure, international conventions had been adopted for protecting prisoners of war and "civilian populations" in territories at
risk or conquered *during wartime* (as in the Geneva Conventions, first formulated in 1864 and then revised and
expanded in 1929, 1949, and 1977). Omitted from that protection, however—as became evident on a broader scale
in World War II than ever before—was protection for
groups of people who either had been residents but were
not citizens of a host country, or had been citizens of that
or another country. The latter groups were then persecuted after either being disenfranchised or found to have
alleged (negative) group-features judged sufficiently dangerous to override rights otherwise granted them. Such
groups, Lemkin saw, were almost entirely without internal protection, since a reigning government could believe
itself entitled to do as it wished to its own populace. This
was the claim made by the Turks in the persecution of the
Armenian minority in Turkey in 1915–17 and by the Nazis
in relation to their own "legal" persecution of the German Jews that began in 1933 and were epitomized in the
disenfranchisement of Jews legislated in the Nuremberg
Laws of 1935: both those attacks were conducted under
the cover of internal legality. Such minority groups, furthermore, were also unprotected *externally* from any
occupying power, since the legal apparatus imposed by
an occupying power could override whatever protection
the occupied country had previously set up; the occupying power could persecute such groups the more readily,
of course, where no such legislation had held.

The concept of genocide verged in this way on a distinctive and novel domain of law, one that breached the

traditional boundaries observed in both national and international law by rejecting the "hands-off" doctrine that gave nations free rein in their treatment of members of their own populace, and one that disputed the premise of international law which granted full standing almost exclusively to nations. The UN Convention on Genocide thus reinforced a conception of *"meta*national" law that would protect groups *aside* from (and sometimes against) the political authority that had formal jurisdiction over them; it extended that protection, furthermore, in peacetime as well as during war. The lengthy theological and philosophical tradition of natural law and natural rights that antedated this development—articulated by such figures as Grotius and John Locke and in such Enlightenment political applications as the US Declaration of Independence (1776) and the French Declaration of the Rights of Man and Citizen (1789)—had been foundational in political and legal thought. But with the rise of modern nationalism, that tradition was seen as also supporting the dualism between intranational and international law, leaving groups that were other or less than full members of nations to fend for themselves. The classic political texts did indeed speak of "natural" and "unalienable"—that is, *inherent*—rights as more fundamental than any granted by national affiliation or citizenship, asserting that every person, apart from the specific character of national citizenship, possessed such rights which *could* then have been extended to associations or groups of citizens within the body politic. In practice, however, those rights, relevant as they were as a rationale for the American and French revolutions, gave way in practice to a less generous model that associated them with the national citizenship of individuals, in effect abandoning groups of citizens qua groups to the space between individual and nation, a space that at the time remained undefended. The "natural" rights asserted were at any rate inherent for individuals *as individuals*, with group associations relevant to that individuality left to fend for themselves, at least so far as the claim of rights was concerned.

It was the members of such groups and the group-formations themselves, unprotected by the law even in otherwise enlightened societies, that Lemkin saw as requiring defense against what he observed historically and then currently as the reality of genocide—the murder or destruction of a group qua group, and by implication then, its members. The act of genocide thus rests equally on the two parts of the term "genocide" itself: "genos" (group), and "cide" (murder). The first of these parts raises more complex conceptual issues than the second (what, after all, *is* a group?), but much needed to be said about the latter as well. Lemkin himself, and then the UN Convention, found, for example, that the destruction of a group did not require that its members be physically killed. A group *could* be destroyed by murder, of course, and this remains the term's most definitive application, with the Nazi genocide against the Jews remaining a paradigm of this. (There could hardly be a more precise expression of genocidal intent than Heinrich Himmler's words to the SS in his Poznan speech of 1943, describing the Nazis' purpose "to make this people [the Jews] disappear from the earth.") But other means would also have the effect of destroying groups of people, and although less immediately cruel, their consequences for group-existence are equally destructive. Thus the UN Convention includes four additional means of genocide: the forcible transfer of children to another group, imposing measures to prevent births within a group, inflicting conditions of life on a group calculated to bring about its destruction, and causing "serious bodily or mental harm" to the members of the group. (In its verdict of September 2, 1998, the UN Tribunal for Rwanda identified under the third of these categories the systematic rape of Tutsi women by the Hutu as a genocidal act, although one could interpret the tribunal's judgment as viewing systematic rape as an independent modality.) These additional means differ in the immediate physical suffering they cause, but it is clear that any of them pursued systematically would conduce to the destruction of the victim-group. And it is clearly this, the demise of the group, the death not only of actual or potential future individual members of the group but of the group as such, that distinguishes the crime of genocide condemned by the UN Convention.

In addition to such differences among possible means of genocide—suggesting the possibility, which it does not itself propose, of also marking "degrees" of genocide—the Convention leaves open or vague its stipulation about the victim of genocidal attack as being a group "in whole or in part." That "in part" phrase has been seized on by critics of the Convention who claim that it implies that the murder of even a single person (who may after all be "part" of a group) would qualify because the person's group-identity, if cited as a cause, would qualify the murder as genocidal. (The phrase's inclusion in the Convention was intended at the time of its adoption to anticipate the murder of the *leadership* "part" of a given group, the effect of which would be to weaken, perhaps fatally, the prospects for group-survival, but that rationale does not solve the problem of ambiguity in the wording.) The need for greater precision in the Convention's wording in this and other instances (this is discussed further in chapters 3 and 4) has been acknowledged by its advocates as well as its critics. Indeed, adjustments of this sort have continually been associated with the Convention through the weight of precedents emerging from actual genocide trials.

Despite the need for such further specification, the crucial principle at the heart of the Convention remains clear and unambiguous: genocide entails the intended destruction of a group, differing in this from the destruction both of individuals and of murder on a large scale—mass murder—where that act is directed at individuals as individuals rather than as members of a collective. Genocide is in this sense not a function of numbers; mass murder that is not genocidal may claim larger numbers of victims than acts of genocide. What is distinctive about the murder in genocide is not the killing of individuals, but murder of the group with the fate of individuals secondary to that intention and its means. As Himmler's statement made explicit, it was against the group of Jews as such that the act of Nazi genocide was directed, if not initially, then ultimately, in what emerged as the "Final Solution of the Jewish Question." Obviously the surest way to destroy a group is by the physical destruction of its individual members, but in genocide that destruction is "only" the means to the supervening end of *group*-destruction.

We find here, then, the distinctive aspect of the evil in genocide: that although it may involve (and has involved) twofold murder, killing at two levels (the murder of individuals as a means to the second "murder" of the group of which the individuals are members), the second level is what distinguishes genocide from individual murder, on the one hand, and from mass murder, on the other. The murder committed in this fashion is directed against two different "beings": individuals, yes, but also, and distinctively, the group of which the individuals are members and from which they draw their identities.

One objection to this formulation may quickly come to mind and has indeed been repeatedly argued. Are not groups only the assembly of a number (an indefinite one, at that) of individuals? How can groups be substantively distinguished from the individuals who constitute them? More will be said about this matter in the following chapters, but a preliminary response draws on the everyday role of groups commonly assumed. Groups—at least, some of them—are not simply individuals added to one other or occupying a particular space. Characteristically, it might be claimed *necessarily*, members of at least some groups occupy a space more complex than and different in status and consequence from the individuals distinguishable within it or even as they might be individually added to each other. In addition to the integrity of their persons, they are part of a corporate or collective "self" closely linked structurally and causally to their individual actions and achievements; their capacities and even inclinations within this collective would be foreign if not impossible for solitary individuals and even for individuals randomly joined. We have only to consider as a rudimentary example of the force of this linkage the "institution" of language, the ability to communicate verbally, as it displays the role—and needs—of a social self. To be sure, groups do not have the *physical* "vital signs" of individual beings, but they constitute lives and histories that infuse and shape the lives and histories of their individual members. And they can also, as the phenomenon of genocide makes clear, suffer death. (The analogy to the threatened deaths of biological species is relevant here—extending also negatively in the sense that political movements in defense of animal species threatened with extinction have rarely been impeded by the question of justification, even as concerns the character of the particular species being protected. Thus, in contrast to the US Senate's forty-year debate before ratifying the UN Genocide Convention, the Senate confirmed the Endangered Species Act of 1977 without dissent and on its first presentation.)

A recurrent issue in the same connection questions also *which* groups are subject to or "eligible for" genocide, since the definition of what counts as a "group" in relation to genocide is itself open. In principle, the number of members required for a group might vary from one to any larger number (Thoreau insisted that any individual person could still be a "majority"). Membership in a group, furthermore, could be based on a variety of indicators, natural or constructed—from eye color or occupation or nationality to the first letter of last names. The UN Convention, however, named only four groups as liable to genocide, based on their special significance in social and cultural life—a restriction that does not mean that the murder of other groups would not be criminal or evil but not, in the Convention's terms, genocidal. There has been and will surely continue to be sharp criticism of the UN Convention for its exclusions here, although more significant is the fact that there has been little disagreement about the groups the Convention *does* name: "national, ethnical, racial or religious groups." The issues that have been raised about these concern the conceptual legitimacy of those categories, not the importance of the four groups in their social roles as those have been perceived either within or from outside the groups themselves.

Why should the four groups named have been singled out for protection? The UN Convention offers no justification or explanation, but the reasoning behind those choices seems prima facie clear, and indeed was presented explicitly in discussions leading up to the adoption of the Convention, as the records of those discussions attest: that the groups named contribute essentially to social structure and life (collective or individual) and have shown this more substantively than most other groups of the multitude that could be named (consider only the possible range here from the College Class of '04 to the residents on Main Street to Sherlock Holmes's "Red-headed League"). There is no stipulation in the Convention that other groups cannot be added to its initial list, and the contentious debates about certain exclusions during the drafting of the Convention and since then might yet lead to specific additions. (The most contentious exclusion seems to have been that of "political" groups or parties, a category excluded from the Convention itself on patently political grounds.) Whatever groups are yet added to the UN list, it seems beyond argument that the four groups named have been significant in shaping cultural and individual identity in contemporary societies: West or East, First World or Third. A test of this claim would be the thought-experiment of imagining what societies or individuals would have been (or be) like without them, with social and individual life then radically different from any familiar to us and difficult even to imagine. The difference there would not be due to the absence of this or that feature in particular individuals, but to the more extensive absence of a *group*-identity as that identity shapes individuals. The effects affecting individuals from this source are arguably at least as strong as those stemming from any other factors, including the innate "givens" of biology.

The primary aspect of the evil in genocide thus comes to this: the types of groups against whom genocide is directed—those *"eligible"* for genocide—are types in whose absence the lives of individuals and collective humanity would have been or would be radically diminished, arguably inconceivable. And so again: the evil is not mainly that genocide may involve individual murder as a means, but that its corporate goal is the destruction of the group-identity without which the individuals would not have been, and could not be, the individuals they were or would be. Genocide in this sense represents the group as in effect a "person," arguably, as Aristotle proposes for the polis in the *Politics*, an entity *prior* to the individual person: life-*giving*, and understood in this way, marking the difference between death and life for the person as something more than biologically individuated. This claim would seem exaggerated if we consider ethnic or religious or national groups and identity as composed of small, discrete parts, a large number of which might be altered or excluded with no *essential* loss—individuals may also "lose" parts of themselves without ceasing to be themselves. But it is important to keep in mind that the destruction intended in genocide is not piecemeal, but total. Murder here, in the first evil of genocide, involves the destruction of the group-means of existence, with that understood to be a condition of personhood.

A second distinguishable feature of the evil in genocide is only obliquely related to the first. This is the intent of genocide to destroy members of a group not because of any act they have been responsible for individually, but solely because of their identification as members of that group. Genocide thus kills individuals not after judging them individually responsible for failing to answer to any specific obligation, but simply because of an identity, with that having been defined to some extent internally among the "membership" but finally, where genocide is enacted, externally, by others. Identification of the group and its members has in this sense typically been determined by the agents of genocide, not by its victims; here as often elsewhere, the social power structure also controls the categories or labels of identity. This process of imposed identification is also, to that extent, arbitrary. So, for one example, the Nazis' definition in the 1935 Nuremberg Laws of who would count as a Jew drew the primary boundary around someone with three Jewish grandparents. That specification, however, was a substantial reduction in the Nazis' ruling concerning Jewish identity issued two years earlier (in the April 7, 1933 Law for the Restoration of the Professional Civil Service) according to which *one* Jewish grandparent sufficed. The basis for that subsequent change, which by the stroke of a pen sharply reduced the total number of "German Jews" (with the irony of that evident), was not biological, and one can only surmise here practical reasons, which in racial terms were, even as the Nazis conceived of the Jews as a race, arbitrary. The earlier, more inclusive definition would have been more costly and difficult to enforce in practice, however odd it may seem that the Nazis would for those reasons find that there could be too many Jews to persecute. Or again, as the process of group-identification comes still closer to absurdity, we recall the alleged (if disputed) policy of the Khmer Rouge of identifying for genocide those of their Cambodian countrymen who wore glasses (not only, but also those), marking them as members of the dangerous group of intellectuals. What happens in these cases is that within the vague initial boundaries of a group marked for genocide, further specifications are characteristically made. These identify group-members neither by their own assent nor for reasons intrinsic to the group-identity itself. Yet they lead with the force of genocide to a death sentence, for infants as well as for those already dying "naturally," for saints as well as sinners.

This grounding of genocide on involuntary identity or character—the denial of individual autonomy—appears also in relation to the question of how individual membership in the four groups named by the UN Convention is determined. For although membership in those groups is voluntary in principle (race traditionally the least so, but also now as the definition of race has been found to be still more a social than a biological category), to a great extent the reality of those identities is involuntary, certainly initially (ethnicity, for example, is transmitted first and strongly through language and home), and then through continuing external pressure and/or external definition. Religion and nationality are more clearly voluntary features of individual identity than the other categories, but for them, too, the pressures *against* "opting out" are often intense, at times overwhelming; many people manage to escape, but others do not, and even for those who do, the process is typically difficult. Also in this respect, then, for those subjected to genocide, the group-identification which is the necessary first step in the process is in the end largely externally imposed. In their loosest applications, these elements of identity are nonetheless distinguishable from other, fuller choices about identity made by members of the group, which means again that genocide acts against its victims on grounds of identifications in whose construction they themselves have little if any part.

To be sure, the justification for genocide by its agents often ascribes to the group attacked responsibility for alleged actions or characteristics of the group's members, claiming that these represent a danger to others, a danger whose source is often alleged to be innate in the group. But even the semblance of evidence for such claims is typically absent; the group attacked is held responsible for dispositions or conduct for which it is not, could not be, responsible, either because the claims are demonstrably false or because the characteristics ascribed to group-members (like physical appearance, as in the differences of complexion) are themselves value-neutral. The starting point here is reflected in the frequency with which the language of genocide turns to medical or biological metaphors: the Jews, in Hitler's own language, were "germ carriers," "a virus," "a racial tuberculosis." This representation of Jews as carriers of disease or the disease itself was then used to justify genocide as surely as the menace of any deadly pestilence would justify its eradication. The justification here is clear: we do not *blame* a virus or bacillus for the harm it causes. The moral issue hardly arises.

Admittedly, societies do act against even involuntary conduct when it appears to be a menace. But such measures are based on individual actions, not on a presumption of group-identity (or conduct), which is at once larger than anything the individual does and also smaller in the sense that there is no necessary connection, where genocide emerges, between the group and the action initiated against it. Genocide, in these terms, adds to the destruction of the group-identity a rejection of the humanity of its victims in denying their autonomy or freedom of decision. They are killed not for choices they have made or acts they have committed, but for alleged dispositions beyond their control or for others on which they might have acted but have not been shown to have done. The actions initiated against them—the genocide—is thus a denial of them as persons, as responsible moral agents— a denial intimated in the twofold murder of genocide, but distinctive enough in this second aspect to stand for itself. In the first facet of the evil in genocide, the denial of the victims' humanity appears as a prior condition or preventative, a declaration that there shall be no such group or individual members of it *in the future*, whereas the second aspect of evil in genocide comes in the denial or reduction of humanity in the group *at present*, as and when it exists. Whatever else can be said against the Nazis' denial that the Jews were human, the internal logic leading to the consequences they inferred from that was rigorous: given their essentialist—pseudo-biological—conception of Jewish group-identity and the number of Jews under their control after their invasions east and west, genocide was not simply the "*Final* Solution"; it became the *only* solution.

If one asks how these two facets of the evil in genocide fit into or reshape the more general conception or understanding of evil, it seems to me that in one way they conform to a standard view, and in another, they challenge it. Both facets conform to a minimalist but standard view of evil as value deliberately negated or destroyed with no sustained justification or commensurate recovery: the destruction affecting not only the potential recognizable in all human beings, but also the *means* (through group-identity) by which, and only by which, that potential can be realized. Genocide, furthermore, also goes beyond this in rejecting one common view of evil which asserts in it an intrinsic relation to ignorance, to an absence of deliberation or intention, by holding that when people do evil or wrong it is not because they chose to do so, cognizant of the evil or wrong in the actions, but because they mistakenly believe that what they are doing is good or at the very least better than the alternative. This rationalist conception (more specifically, denial) of evil figures largely in Plato and the Platonic tradition, in the seventeenth-century Enlightenment thought of Spinoza and Leibniz, and at least in one strand of the Judeo-Christian tradition—if people who do evil only knew better, if they *really* understood what they were doing, they would not do it.

There is much to be said, and much that has been said, about—for and against—this view of evil. Some of what is at issue here was dramatically brought face-to-face with the occurrence of genocide in Hannah Arendt's analysis of Adolf Eichmann's character and role in the "Final Solution," familiar through her phrase the "banality of evil": the claim that Eichmann managed to do great evil although neither his intention nor he himself was at all "great." He was no Iago, Arendt claims, no Richard III; he did not think enough about what he was doing to qualify as authentically, and certainly not radically, evil; indeed, he hardly thought at all. He was—in her words— "thoughtless," a "clown," who unfortunately found himself (he spoke of his own "bad luck") in a position that placed fateful decisions in his hands. That thoughtlessness, Eichmann's reliance on clichés not only in speaking but in *thinking*, was his, and his evil's, banality. A clear implication of Arendt's account is that if Eichmann *had* been capable of thought, he would not have done what he did. Iago and Richard III, after all, in the forms that we know them best, are products of Shakespeare's imagination; there and there only, we might infer from Arendt's account, is where radical evil, evil deliberately chosen, is to be found—in fictional worlds, not in ordinary human agency and responsibility. She had come to realize, Arendt concluded not long after the Eichmann book's appearance, in a letter to Gershom Scholem, that "*all* evil is banal." (I elaborate on this reversal in Arendt's view in chapter 8.)

Insofar as this alleged impossibility of voluntary or willed evil is at all open to verification, the phenomenon of genocide seems to me to provide certain counterevidence to, at the very least, raise serious doubts about it. For it is a feature of genocide as conceived in the UN Convention that it is always intentional, and although in this respect, genocide may seem no different from other premeditated acts, an implication of what I have been saying is that genocidal intention is not only directed at the destruction of the group but aims at that destruction in full knowledge of the act's wrongfulness. In other words, those who commit genocide both recognize the wrong and do what they do at least in part for that reason, in effect making that knowledge itself an element of the intention. This is obviously a large claim to justify, whether for genocide in general or for its specific instances (or for any other wrong). I have elsewhere attempted to show how an awareness of their wrongdoing figured in the Nazis' "Final Solution," arguing that the moral quality of that process appears in the conscious "style" of Nazi expression and actions where, in addition to their specific wrongdoing, the conscious will to transgression itself is also evident.

I rehearse my argument for this claim only in abbreviated form here, relating it as well to the still more difficult challenge of proving that genocide as such—as an institution of war—involves conscious wrongdoing, consciousness not only of the act of group-murder but also of the evil in it. On the latter point, I would argue that the rationale for killing on the basis of an imposed group-identity always betrays itself. It can never be undertaken in good faith because of the disproportion between the object and the act: it is the group traits that are condemned, but it is individuals in whom the traits may be absent or at least not evident who are killed. And the disparity between those two, no matter how much effort is made to align them, cannot be reconciled or resolved. This claim is supported by certain apparently accidental, albeit typical features of genocide which are, in my view, not accidental at all: the invariable practice of secrecy and denial on the part of those carrying it out; the elaborate—and one has to say, imaginative—efforts at dehumanization which typically accompany it (not simply direct physical or brute torture but measures directed against the person as a member of the "genos"); and the parallel compartmentalization characteristic in its agents' actions and affect. All these features of genocide require explanation, and one such explanation points to an awareness of the evil being committed on the part of those doing it. Some of the features mentioned may figure in any atrocity or even lesser instances of wrongdoing, but the requirement in genocide of imposing and then annihilating group-identity intensifies both the occasion and the need for a consciousness of the transgression.

I realize that the broad thesis of intentional and knowing wrongdoing (inside or outside genocide) requires more evidence and argument than I provide here, but even its possibility is important as a basis for questioning the view that wrongdoing can never be fully voluntary—a basis to which genocide adds its weight in as distinctive a way as genocide itself is distinctive in its history.

At the beginning of this chapter, I suggested an alternative title that might have seemed offensive, and I would balance that now, in concluding, by proposing still another possible source of offence: that along with what has been described here as the evil in genocide, we would do well also to look for the good in it. The immediate response to such a proposal will undoubtedly be, "No good has ever come or could come out of genocide, no redeeming features, none!" But a more considered response involves looking at one historical aspect of the conceptualization of genocide which indeed promises—I think of no other way of describing them—positive or even good consequences. In an age of social self-consciousness, the relationship between immoral practice and moral prohibition hardly needs retelling. Even the skepticism of a writer like Montaigne would remind us that one thing we know when we read in history about various religious or cultural prohibitions or taboos is that practices identified as stigmatized and prohibited have in fact occurred—and with sufficient frequency to be regarded as a danger. There would be no prohibitions against murder, robbery, adultery, and incest unless they had first been part of the moral (or immoral) landscape—unless they had occurred. Furthermore, for all these prohibitions and their attendant punishments, something more seems to be going on than only the delineation of individual offenses.

What occurs here seems also a stirring of the moral imagination which in some way anticipates specific violations and prohibitions but comes into full view only as the pair—act and prohibition together—appear. Together, they then shape further the extent of the moral domain which, it should by now be clear, has a history that is even in its own qualified way a progressive history. This is not to say that wrongs as they are singled out and identified *become* good or right in the process, or that, if we had the choice, it would not be right or good (whatever that might mean in this context) to prefer a world without both the stigmatized act and the prohibition found in reaction against it—a world from which evil and the moral imagination reacting to it would be absent—but only that in *this* world (ours), wrong or evil can be, and sometimes are, met by right and good. And that in itself is good.

Something like this sequence has appeared, I would argue, in relation to genocide as it has been conceptualized, identified, and then expressed in legal, moral, and common discourse. For a concurrent event has been the emergence, also in legal, moral, and common discourse, of "group-rights": the concept of the rights of groups (first and foremost) to exist, to *be* groups—that is, of self-determination—but also extending from that to other rights implied by or built on that first one. The contemporaneous recognition of genocide as a crime and of group-rights as a condition of moral and political justice that emerged in the aftermath of World War II is not, *could not*, be accidental: they are too closely related conceptually and chronologically, too much history had passed with neither of them identified for their simultaneous emergence to be coincidental. Even if one sees the historical progression as moving first from the crime of genocide to recognition of the new group-right to exist—first, violation, then virtue or justice—there is nothing startling in this; much, perhaps all, moral history follows a similar pattern. Admittedly, all talk of "group-rights" faces substantial objections, but so, after all, does talk of *individual* rights (which, we recall, the utilitarian philosopher Jeremy Bentham caustically challenged as "nonsense upon stilts"). A common presumption has always been, furthermore, that if group-rights are acknowledged at all, they emerge only as individual rights bundled together: since I as an individual have the right to free speech, so, too, any group of which I am a member (together with other individuals) has the same right, but only because of the individual rights of its individual members. But an alternate view of the concept of group-rights raises the possibility that group-rights may on certain issues precede rather than follow individual rights, or at least that the two may be cotemporal or cological. The concept also proposes a "deep structure" for society quite different from the individualist conception of human nature and social structure deeply embedded in contemporary Western political ideology.

In certain respects, the practice of group-rights has advanced more quickly than its theory, since many aspects of contemporary political life—from issues of affirmative action to church-state relations to questions of property rights and taxation—seem dependent not only on the possibility but on the actuality of group-rights. This connection, however, is a topic warranting its own consideration, and I mention it not to divert attention from this chapter's central focus on genocide but to show that even in relation to that extreme act, moral history and analysis do not escape the reach of dialectic. Certainly the appearance of group-rights as underwriting the identification and criminalizing of genocide is not meant as a concluding "uplift" to the terrible story of genocide which remains, I would argue, a (if not *the*) dominant moral motif of twentieth century history. But the two sides have arrived close together, and so, in the end, they also have to be viewed together. Group-rights, yes—because *first*, group wrongs. And at the beginning of that beginning, genocide.

Genocide and Comparative Evil

Counting Victims, Numbers, Degrees

It is a truth universally acknowledged that some wrongful acts are more wrongful than others. Why is this? That is, why the universal acknowledgment, and before that, why the "truth" itself? I address these questions first because every instance of recognized wrongdoing presupposes answers to those more general formulations. How, after all, could we distinguish wrongful from rightful acts without assurance from moral history (not the history of ethical *theory*, but the history of ethical *practice*) that the fact of moral distinctions, specifically of distinctions among acts of violence or other means of harm, has a basis in reason? Ideally such assurance would establish not only the possibility but the necessity of moral judgment through gradations of value (or, inverting the order, gradations of disvalue), and we do indeed find this practice in the history of valuation itself.

What are the specific steps in the gradations of wrongful acts, and how are those distinctions made? This second, in many ways more dramatic, set of issues bears on specific comparisons through the measurement of "evil"—for example, in comparing the numbers of deaths caused or by distinguishing manners or intensity or degrees of intention. The practical difficulties in sustaining such comparisons are greater than those raised by the question of the status of those comparisons in principle, but this problem seems due more to excessive demands on the process of measurement than to the measurements themselves. Aristotle's warning that we are entitled to require in a science or method only the degree of precision of which it is capable can be self-serving (or self-deceiving), but in this instance it seems a cogent response to the common objection that because moral comparisons seem in the end always either imprecise or underdetermined, even to attempt them is obscurantist or mystifying. But quite the contrary: Comparison is at the heart of moral judgment and assessment. There is no right without a wrong, no justice without injustice, no prohibition without (prior) violation: whatever the intrinsic slippage in specific comparisons, that fault pales beside the necessity for them.

A few words first about my claim of universal acknowledgment of the *principle* of discrimination among degrees or kinds of wrongdoing. This principle holds that wrongs come in—certainly are known by—degrees of "wrongfulness" (i.e., of what it is that makes them wrong), and that at least some of the moral differences distinguished by way of these degrees are so clear and significant that the principle has been generally, arguably universally, recognized.

If this claim seems overstated, it is not so by much. The one quasi-historical counterexample that comes to mind remains a solitary exception. This deviant instance is the Code of Draco, dated to about 621 BCE, of whose history few details survive but which itself has become emblematic of a distinctive manner of justice. "Draconian" laws now typically refer to laws that are exceptionally harsh, but their essential conceptual feature initially was not their severity but their denial of all difference between lesser and greater transgressions. One punishment for all crimes was Draco's rule, on the grounds that there was a common wrong committed in them all, one and the same—namely, that they were all, equally, violations of the law. As it also happened, the uniform punishment imposed by the Draconian Code was harsh: death. Hence the association of "draconian" with severity, although viewed conceptually, the reference is less a commitment to a specific punishment than to the extent of its reach. By contrast, at least for the past three hundred years, most legal systems that sanction capital punishment have typically reserved it for only certain crimes which they specify, distinguishing in this way what they take to be greater offenses from lesser ones—a distinction invisible on the Draconian view. "Small offenses," Draco is said to have held, "deserve death, and I can think of no more severe penalty for larger ones."

How Draco himself arrived at his conclusion is unknown, but the principle underlying his harsh and brief table of laws—his theory of justice—is clear. If we think of justice as the application of statutory law or as invoking the good as viewed through moral obligation (or both), then every violation is equivalent to every other one insofar as it *is* a violation. To be sure, the grounds cited for determining the relevant norms or prohibitions vary—as expressions of natural law, rules of state or conscience, the word of God, or more simply, social conventions. But so long as the norm applied has some such authority, transgressions have the common feature of violating whatever in that community of discourse commands obedience. Because all violations are then equal as violations, the argument would go, there is no basis for differential punishment. (Again, determining what the particular uniform punishment should *be* is conceptually and practically distinct from the claim that punishment for all violations should be uniform; the latter is the equivalent of a moral "flat tax" with the uniform rate still to be determined.)

There have been few, if any, advocates of the latter view after Draco himself, whether among political theorists or rulers in fact. It might be argued that for consistency's sake, Kant should have been a draconian—and certainly there is an echo in Kant of Draco's unflinching (categorical?) view of the inviolability of all moral law. But Kant did not in fact sustain that position with Draconian consistency, arguing against it for proportionality or "fit" between a crime and its punishment rather than holding the one-size (of punishment)-fits-all view. The distinctiveness of the Draconian Code, furthermore, is evident not only among the practices or designs of other *individual* rulers or theorists but more importantly, among political bodies as such; no states or societies with even a putative table of laws have refused or failed to identify certain transgressions as more wrongful than others. This hierarchical ordering of moral and/or legal violations is then a genuine "cultural universal," although rarely noted as that; it is accepted and practiced among otherwise very different cultures, although the specific rankings of values or prohibitions (and the proportionate punishments) vary among them. About the latter variations, the evidence is clear. So, for example, the death penalty is mandated biblically for violating the Sabbath by so superficially minor an act as picking up and moving a piece of wood from one place to another, but not for bodily harm of a person that stops short of actual killing—a distinctive hierarchy of judgment. But such intercultural differences do not affect the claim of universality for the universal *intra*cultural phenomenon of the recognized gradations among moral offenses.

The explanation for this widespread differential pattern may seem self-evident: *of course*, there is a difference between killing and wounding, between lying and ordering a campaign of extermination, with such differences translated directly into legal distinctions and then into gradations of punishment. But for fundamental ethical principles as they have been practiced, there is no "of course" (of course). Further explanation is required, and the most obvious place to look for that is in a combination of the intentions and the consequences connected to the actions being judged. Thus, where human life is regarded as a good, murder would be a more serious offense than an assault which leaves the victim alive: *attempted* murder. Even punishment that itself involves the taking of a life may be held—ironically, it might seem—to reflect the high value attached to life; the thirty-eight states of the United States that as of this writing retain the option of capital punishment also restrict that punishment to specific types or acts of murder. Nowhere is capital punishment sanctioned as a punishment for speeding or illegal parking, although it is almost certainly true that in contrast to the apparently nondeterrent effect of capital punishment for murder, capital punishment for speeding or illegal parking would indeed reduce their occurrence.

And the obvious reason for this discrimination in punishment is the differing proportions of the combination of harm caused and the intention behind it that figure in the violations.

The principle applied here—the basis for its commitment to differential punishment—is some variant of the dictum that "the punishment should fit the crime," advocating proportionality between the acts of crime and their respective punishments. That principle in turn rests on two assumptions: first, that punishments differ in severity (by an independent standard that has turned out to vary from culture to culture); and second, that crimes differ in *their* severity—in whatever it is that makes the crime a crime. Fitting a punishment to the crime argues for proportionality between the two sides which is thus dependent on measurements assigned to each. Such proportionality, moreover, appears not only warranted but required—that is, as a moral requirement, with the implication that either excessive or deficient punishments themselves become moral wrongs. To be sure, an act's consequences are not the only factors warranting consideration in assessing crimes and their related punishments—intentions are usually also considered relevant, at times decisively—and it is not only the difference between utilitarianism and deontology that affects the choice here. In the common distinction in US law between murder and manslaughter, for instance, the consequences of the wrong committed are identical: a wrongful death. It is the intention (or its absence) underlying the act that determines the differing judgments of the agent's actions and, subsequently, of the punishment mandated. Philosophical views of the elements of moral judgment have typically been more "purist" than those of legal systems in defining those elements—thus the Kantian straightforward exclusion of consequences as relevant to moral assessment, balanced at the other end of the spectrum by the utilitarian or consequentialist counterclaim of the flat irrelevance of intentions. Even with such far-reaching differences, however, the systems in common distinguish between more and less serious transgressions; on that point, they are at one, again supporting the principle of proportionality.

In this sense, comparative assessments seem intrinsic to moral judgment, and certainly they have been in constant attendance. Only consider the world as it would be without moral gradations, even with simply the Manichaean dualism of good and evil (of which Draco's Code was an instance), and we find an unrecognizable and in practical terms an uninhabitable world that contrasts sharply with the familiar world of common moral experience in which grays occur much more frequently than blacks or whites. In other words, the branches of the tree of the knowledge of good and evil—the distinctions *within* those concepts—are as significant as the basic distinction itself; indeed, they finally *constitute* that distinction. This consideration applies, I should argue, not only to degrees of wrongdoing but also to gradations of the good, although the focus of moral and certainly legal analyses has been mainly on the former. The category of supererogatory acts—heroic deeds that go beyond what is required on the side of the good—marks a degree in "right-doing" beyond obligation but remains still within the hierarchy of moral judgment.

Nevertheless, it seems clear that these graded distinctions, however relevant in sustaining moral judgment, pose serious difficulties in practice—especially where wrongdoing involves irreparable harm to human life and still more as the number of human lives affected increases. In one obvious sense, the difference between the murder of ten thousand people and that of a single person seems indisputable, a conclusion which becomes still more compelling when the number of victims reaches into the millions. The twentieth century provides remarkable examples of the latter extension in the actions of Nazi Germany and the Soviet Union during the periods of their power. A large moral issue that arises as soon as a comparison between those two "examples" is undertaken is the question of how, or even whether, comparisons can be measured in moral terms between or among what are recognized as moral atrocities. Is numerical computation a legitimate key in such comparison? That is, do two murders count as twice the wrong of a single murder (ignoring any question about *who* was murdered, which would itself, as a question, pose a moral issue), two million as twice the wrong of one million, and so on? Would the agent's guilt and wrongdoing in such occurrences be similarly tabulated? For the advocates of utilitarianism or consequentialism, a "felicific" calculus based on the tabulation of lives lost (assuming other considerations to be equal) would be the only criterion a judge could require or appeal to in reaching a judgment of moral value in such differences. Prima facie, however, this computational view of ethical judgment, whether on a large or small scale, seems crude, even *im*moral—the more so because the calculus applied offers no intrinsic reason for giving human lives primacy when compared to other social goods of the living; it might be (and has been) held that lives can justifiably be sacrificed in order to increase the well-being or even on some accounts the pleasure of a larger number of others.

Is there an alternative to this theory for which numbers alone are not decisive? In fact, there is no need here to concede the either/or as has traditionally been assumed, since the two extremes themselves—ethics by the numbers or ethics by pure form—suggest a third way which takes each into account in proposing a means of reconciling them. This possibility surfaced earlier here in my reference to the contrast between the crimes of manslaughter and murder and by analogy provides a basis for a similar distinction between mass murder and genocide. If we recognize the biblical Cain (figuratively if not literally) as responsible for the first murder (then as that act's "inventor"), we find even in the brief course of biblical history an extension to murder in larger numbers, although still and most often the murder of individuals as individuals, reaching sometimes (as in the destruction of the cities of Sodom and Gomorrah) mass proportions. An intimation of killing along a different axis, however, also emerges in the biblical reference to the Amalekites, whose individual members and their descendants if there are any—thus the group as such—are all to be destroyed. In a remarkable extension, the reach of obliteration there is commanded to include wiping out also the *memory* of Amalek. (The commandment to remember to wipe out a memory has its own problems, but the enormity of the intention here is evident.)

With this prescription, and leaving aside the issue of motivation or cause impelling the act or the related issues of theodicy where God appears as an agent, the

conceptual distinction between mass murder and genocide emerges fully formed, although in its twentieth century appearances, the character of genocide in its fullest
force as a double murder—that of individuals *and* of a
group—extends farther and is still more open to public
scrutiny. The break or elaboration that genocide marks in
the analysis of culpable killing (i.e., murder) represents
a development (in a perverse sense, progress) in moral
history: first in the evolution of actions that are morally
significant for conceptualizing the phenomenon of evil—
comparable in this to the first individual murder perpetrated by Cain—and then as the history of moral acts is
itself elaborated and conceptualized: a pattern of progress
in ethical analysis.

I attempt later in this book to address the systematic issues involved in this concern for the lives of groups
(e.g., the need to define the status of groups in relation
to that of individuals as against the nominalist tradition in political philosophy and metaphysics for whom
the very existence of groups is derivative, even illusory
or epiphenomenal). And then too, the question has continually to be faced of *which* groups are to be recognized
as potential victims of genocide, given the need for some
principle of selection (the number of potentially "privileged" groups is large enough to block any understanding of the concept of genocide without such a principle).
Again, the overriding contribution to moral assessment
that "genocide" makes is the distinction it both assumes
and asserts in going beyond using only the counting of
numbers in judging the wrong of instances of premeditated or intentional murder. To be sure, responsibility for
a million deaths looms larger in moral enormity than the

murder of a single person. But as soon as this is said, the reminder is unavoidable of how wrongful *individual* murder is. Sentencing a serial killer to four or five "life terms" may serve a symbolic purpose (a number of *death sentences* passed on a murderer would become a parody rather than a symbol), but it does not resolve the moral issue here. Nor do the conventional formulas by which damages for "wrongful death" are assigned in terms of economic loss even pretend to provide a moral finding of the degree of wrong ascribed to the responsible act or agent. None of these attempts, furthermore, and however one judges them otherwise, detracts from the qualitative distinction introduced in the concept of genocide between types of murder on a mass scale. The difference between the murder of a million people and that of a single person is obvious in its consequences (also in the premeditation required by the former and possibly present or not in relation to the other). But that difference by itself does not constitute a moral distinction applicable to either the agent(s) or the act, underscoring again that numbers do not in themselves resolve the issue of how moral comparisons at that level are to be made.

On the other hand, moral differences by *degrees* of wrongdoing are both measurable and relevant in relation to the moral judgment of murder, and the distinction between degrees and numbers then also becomes evident. The number of victims of an act of mass murder may be larger than the number of victims of a genocide, as there may be more victims of an accident caused by a drunken driver and thus guilty of manslaughter than the premeditated murder of a single victim. But just as in the latter case it is not the number of victims that determines the

differing judgments (and punishments) of those responsible, so also in relation to the difference between mass
murder and genocide, it is not the question of whether
the acts are intended or premeditated that distinguishes
them: mass murder may also be premeditated, but the
intention then acted on is not directed against the group
of which its victims are members. Even within genocide,
moreover, the possibility, indeed the need, of degrees or
gradations which override the issues of numbers or per-
centages is evident (and may eventually be included in the
conceptualization of genocide). The UN Convention on
Genocide justifiably recognizes the prevention of births
within a group as a form of genocide because if such prevention were fully implemented, the victim-group would
disappear in a generation's time. But there is nonetheless a
substantive difference between this attack and the physical murder of a group of living persons.

Where does this leave the question of comparability
between the actions of Nazi Germany and Soviet Russia,
in the horrendous examples each set? Confining ourselves
to counting and comparing the number of victims, I have
been arguing, although not morally irrelevant, is also not
the sole consideration for moral judgment of those examples. The number of Soviet victims, even before World
War II, is generally recognized as larger than the number of victims for which Nazi policies and actions were
responsible. (If more examples were needed, one might
juxtapose the number of Mao's victims, arguably larger
than either of these other two). Mass murder does not
have the goal of the full extermination of a group, whereas
in genocide that goal need not be realized for the charge
of genocide to apply—an important point of difference in

genocide from homicide which is sharply distinguished from "attempted" homicide. That the Nazis failed in their attempt at genocide in no way diminishes the charge against them; the failure was not due to a lack of will or effort as evidenced in what they actually did. The argument has been made that the deliberate famine initiated in Ukraine by the Soviets in 1932–33 which claimed up to five million lives should be recognized as genocide, that the Soviet dispersion of the Chechens to Kazakhstan and the cultural suppression of the Tatars should be similarly categorized under the definition of genocide in the UN Convention.

The issues contested in categorizing these events may finally move in one direction or the other but what in any event cannot be avoided is the distinction cited here between mass murder and genocide—a macabre distinction, and yet significant if it is sustained. There is substantial evidence that the famine in the Ukraine was knowingly imposed by the Soviet regime, with part of that knowledge the probable, at least approximate, cost in lives that the famine would exert. There is also evidence that the identity of the famine's victims among the Ukrainian peasantry was a factor in its being directed against them. But the magnitude of the atrocity is in no way diminished by recognizing that the famine was part of one that extended elsewhere in the USSR, and that in the Ukraine itself was motivated not by the aim of exterminating all the ethnic Ukrainians but as directing a problem of food supplies at the Ukraine in the knowledge that the problem could have been confronted very differently. This account of the Soviet intention has been contested, with the famine characterized as indeed genocidal, but I introduce the contrast between it and the Nazis' "Final Solution of the Jewish Question" about which, aside from the phenomenon of Denial, there has been little debate about its role as genocide. Also the Nazi genocide against the Jews included an economic motive, but the intention in principle of "making [that] people disappear"—a full recipe for genocide—was the binding ligature of the Nazi purpose. It is not necessary to judge one or the other of these atrocities as more or less morally horrific either before or after recognizing the difference in clarity of intention and then in form that distinguishes the two.

What bearing this or any such moral distinction has in assessing the comparative structures of the two systems from which they sprang or in articulating the concept of totalitarianism more generally is a separate question, and it should be clear that the distinction provides no cover for totalitarianism, however that form of political rule expresses its intrinsic reliance on force. Nor does it rule out the possibility that at some point in moral history, a radically different system of measurement may be required, along the lines of the philosopher Jean-Francois Lyotard's contention that the enormity of twentieth century history as exemplified in the Holocaust broke the previously adequate instruments of moral measurement, making clear the need for new ones. Whether such a recalibration is needed or even possible remains in question, but the event to which Lyotard's formulation responds, with its historicization of moral wrongdoing as it brings that event too into history, is significant. Much of that recalibrating would turn on the conceptualization of genocide and its incorporation into legislative, moral, and common discourse. Obviously nothing in that process would add anything positive to the phenomenon of genocide itself. But given the fact of its past occurrence and the ominous prospect of its future, any advance in its conceptualization will be at once a purpose and an achievement in the defense of "genocide."

Disputing "Genocide"

Issues of Uniqueness and Group-Identity

The pushback against the concept of genocide as a moral, legal, and historical category marks the concept's coming of age, since criticism of it seems to have increased (certainly to be sustained) simultaneously with its increasing influence and effect. Issues of minority rights in the first half of the twentieth century—beginning even prior to the Versailles treaty after the end of World War I and its related international jurisprudence, followed by the political and social realignments of minority populations in the subsequent interwar period and *then* by the Nazi genocide of the Jews in World War II—converged in the adoption by the UN General Assembly of the Convention on the Prevention and Punishment of the Crime of Genocide. In the half century after that, the concept of genocide achieved a presumptive place in legislative, political, and public discourse; those force lines culminated in the 1998 Rome Statute, passed by 120 states, which founded the International Criminal Court that held its opening session in March 2003 after the Rome Statute's ratification by the requisite sixty signatories. A specific, although not exclusive, charge to the ICC which meets now in The Hague is the prosecution and punishment of the crime of genocide. For that court, as well as for the ad hoc International Criminal Tribunals established previously under the aegis of the United Nations to investigate specific atrocity sites (such as the former Yugoslavia and Rwanda), judicial scrutiny of the crime of genocide has been a distinctive purpose.

This progression of the concept of genocide to a normative role in jurisprudence and public discourse has not, however, been uncontested. In the United Nations itself, in the process leading up to the 1948 adoption of the Genocide Convention, the crucial definition of "genocide," the concept's applications and means, provoked sharp disagreement. Certain issues that were raised then and either acted on to nobody's full satisfaction or simply left unresolved have remained, intensified by the Convention's spare formulation which included what have come to be recognized as instances of ambiguity, arbitrariness, even inconsistency—at least some of which have been acknowledged as much by the Convention's defenders as by its critics. Despite such reservations, the Genocide Convention is nonetheless still generally deferred to as the authoritative formal statement on genocide. Although the Convention's applicability to particular events has at times been disputed—that is, whether the Convention's definition of genocide applied to a particular set of events—those disagreements have been directed not at the concept of genocide as the Convention defined it as a crime, but on its applicability to specific set of events. (So, for example, the still ongoing debate concerning the Serbian atrocities in the Bosnian War of 1992–95. In 2005, the US Congress passed a resolution characterizing the Serbian role in that war as genocide, but the International Criminal Tribunal on the Former Yugoslavia considering the same events both before and after 2005 has reached conflicting judgments on this.) Such disputes about the interpretation and application of laws are not unusual for regulations or laws of much longer standing; the distinction between the implementation of laws and the intended reach of the laws themselves is evident.

This general acceptance of the Convention on Genocide has been driven by external circumstances as well as by its own claims. Its origins were impelled strongly by the still fresh reaction in 1948 to the Nazi genocide of the Jews which would remain a paradigm for the conceptualization of that atrocity. To this immediate association was added the fact that many countries, including smaller member countries of the United Nations, had national memories of atrocity from their own histories that predated World War II and which now found expression in support for the Convention. (Raphael Lemkin was to draw heavily on that source in his efforts for the Convention's approval by the UN General Assembly, looking especially to the countries of Central and South America.) And then, too, later than those originary factors, large-scale atrocities *post*–World War II (in Cambodia, Bosnia, Rwanda) have approximated closely *enough* the terms of the UN Convention to mute if not to resolve challenges to the concept; the murders in the atrocities themselves were understandably the focus of attention. And finally, there has been a continuing sense of *faute de mieux*: recognition that attempts to nullify or even to amend the UN Convention would open a Pandora's box, adding as many additional problems and disagreements as those that could be resolved.

This balance has changed recently, however, with a growing number of objections to the term and concept of "genocide." Such objections vary in their emphases, although it should be noted that "genocide-denial" *as such* has virtually no place among them. The common issues raised by critics focus not on the question of whether atrocities, and thus serious crimes, were committed in the events labeled as "genocide," but whether the designation of "genocide" could not itself be improved on: formulated under other rubrics more precisely, more consistently, more fully aligned with legal practice and understanding and with fewer conceptual problems—for example, as "crimes against humanity" or "crimes against peace" or "war crimes."

Two books published in the last decade—Marc Nichanian's *The Historiographic Perversion* (2009) and Larry May's *Genocide: A Normative Account* (2010)—contributed to this pushback and are in a number of ways representative. Both Nichanian and May proposed—on different grounds and with proportionately different consequences—to minimize and finally to displace the concept of genocide. "Genocide" articulated first in English in Raphael Lemkin's coinage (a term used then also in other languages that adopted it, or its approximate translation) appears in the formulations of Nichanian and May as no more than a makeshift term applied to then current or recent events, one that has since, however, been given iconic—but also confused and confusing—status. For the standard definition of "genocide" reveals itself, according to these critics, as faulty in a number of significant ways, appearing now as an archaism still in current usage but no more relevant than "aether" would be in designating the earth's atmosphere. "Genocide," in their analyses, is best understood as one aspect or instance of other crimes rather than as pointing to an independent referent. And this is because the term is historically and conceptually muddled and vague in a number of its key claims or presuppositions.

There is ample reason for taking such criticism seriously. That the concept of genocide is not self-evident is itself evident in the history of genocide prior to the term's coining. Lemkin found instances of genocide in the Hebrew Bible and classical Greece and Rome, and argued for his neologism on the grounds that it answered an unmet need in international law to protect otherwise defenseless groups of people both within and across national boundaries. In response to that statement of purpose, critics of "genocide," like the several discussed here and in the following chapter, have in effect posed three counterclaims: (1) that no such need exists; (2) that the concept of genocide as originally formulated and still accepted does not meet the need—if there *is* one— adequately; and (3) that other legal or moral concepts meet the need more fully or precisely. Neither Marc Nichanian nor Larry May supports the first option—an important consideration in the logic of their positions, since it seems to grant the existence, arguably even also the right to exist, of certain groups. To be sure, Nichanian then enters restrictive stipulations about what can be known or said *about* groups, at least when they are attacked genocidally, and May so strongly limits the sense in which groups can be said to exist at all as to raise questions about the consistency between his positive proposals and his nominalist assumptions. To note the problems found in these two critiques of both genocide and "genocide" does not itself constitute a blanket defense of what Nichanian and May are attacking (formally, the Genocide Convention's formulation), but they are sufficiently basic to be relevant for any defense of it.

Nichanian's book is impelled by the fate of the Armenian populace in Turkey during the years before and during World War I—an occurrence for which Nichanian emphasizes the Armenian designation, the "Aghed" ("Catastrophe") rather than what he regards as the obscurantist "Armenian Genocide," the reference usually cited. His opposition to the designation of "genocide" evolved for him from two "affairs" in France. The first was the 1994 trial in Paris of the American historian Bernard Lewis on charges of "negationism": denial of the occurrence of the Armenian genocide. The second was the candidacy in 1999 of the historian Gilles Veinstein for a position at the College de France that provoked a public controversy (although no legal charges) stemming from his 1994 essay supporting Lewis's position: Veinstein, too, was accused of "negationism." (The ruling was not enforced retroactively, but the French parliament in 1998 had formally declared that the Armenians *were* victims of genocide.) An array of French intellectuals defended Veinstein, including several with whom Nichanian had previously felt intellectual kinship (for instance, Pierre Vidal-Naquet and Jacques Derrida), but with whom he now took issue. Lewis was found guilty by the French court and fined one franc; Veinstein was subsequently confirmed in the College position by a slim majority (18–15, with two abstentions)—but both outcomes posed more questions for Nichanian than they resolved. Indeed, the controversies led him to the conclusion he states at the beginning of his book and repeats as a refrain: "Genocide is not a fact."

What this conclusion means and how Nichanian supports it provide the main thrust of his book. The Bernard Lewis trial was occasioned by an interview in *Le Monde* (November 16, 1993) in which Lewis, avoiding an answer to the question of why the Turkish government "refuses to recognize the Armenian genocide," maintained that although what occurred was a "horrible human tragedy," there was "no serious proof of a decision . . . [by] the Ottoman government regarding the extermination of the Armenian nation." As Nichanian points out, the guilty verdict reached by the court itself avoided the issue of "negationism" (i.e., "denial"), faulting Lewis simply for not having adequately presented "the elements contrary to his thesis." (One can only imagine the number of criminal judgments requiring the attention of the court systems if *that* criterion were applied to all historical narratives.)

The grounds for these outcomes and for the Gayssot Law of 1990 on which they drew can be disputed, but they are not the basis of Nichanian's rejection of "genocide," the term or the concept in its specific application to the Aghed. Partly from outrage that there might be any doubt about the nature of the Turks' actions against their Armenian minority, partly as the outcome of a minimal argument, Nichanian draws the sweeping conclusion that "genocide is not a fact," building on what he sees as a clear distinction between fact and interpretation: if one, not the other—if the other, not the one. If the Aghed's occurrence is *only* a matter of interpretation, then any claim of its historicity will be as contestable as it's contradictory, and this, on Nichanian's view, *cannot be* the case: if anything is real, the Aghed was, is. Why, then, can the Aghed—or genocide in any other of its appearances—*not* be a "fact"? For Nichanian, the decisive element separating interpretation from fact is the role of intention in the former. And he (accurately) understands Lewis's argument against ascribing genocide to the Turkish attacks as based on Lewis's contention, valid or not, that no *intention* of genocide on the part of the Turks has been proven. (Lewis was adhering strictly to the Genocide Convention's stipulation that any charge of genocide must include sufficient evidence of the intention to commit that act.)

But why, according to Nichanian, must any reference to intention go beyond facts? He seems to view this claim as self-evident: since intention is a matter of interpretation, it *cannot* be factual. Why not? Because any conclusion that requires an inference based on intention is open to at least the possibility of denial or at least dispute—and for the Aghed, in his view, this possibility would itself disqualify the claim. The Paris court had had its say about Bernard Lewis, and the French intellectual community had had their say about Gilles Veinstein—but neither process nor their outcome did justice to the Aghed. One might conclude then that the Aghed is for Nichanian stronger a fact than is recognized in the common understanding of what facts are: it is to be not only true but undeniable, having the force of a "factual a priori." Assertions of fact are typically, even when generally accepted, regarded as deniable at least in principle, and this applies to them whether they appear by reference to intention or not. What, then, *is* the status of the Aghed on Nichanian's terms? The one remaining possibility—aside from the power of the court that holds the Aghed to be a "fact" simply to *enforce* its verdict—would be that the Aghed is nonpareil, a unique occurrence, beyond reach of disconfirmation and so also of verification. Nichanian hints here that what is known as "the Holocaust" is similarly situated beyond interpretation (or denial), and one might infer from these claims, as taken together, that still other occurrences characterized as genocide might also warrant the same claim of uniqueness—not only each of them, but then arguably all of them viewed together under the concept of genocide, which presumably then would appear undermined together, if they were presented together in a "factual" account of genocide generalized from its instances.

Nichanian traces his own view of the Aghed largely to evidence of personal testimony from contemporary Armenian accounts or later testimony from survivors— some from his family, some from other sources. He barely mentions the contentious truth status of eyewitness testimony although he seems familiar with the debates about that status since he takes the trouble to draw *also* on extra-testimonial sources. In any event, the basis of Nichanian's line of argument remains the radical division he posits between interpretation and fact and the dependence of intention on the former. He nowhere considers the extensive legal and philosophical literature on intention—a considerable omission even if he found nothing there that might cause him to alter his positivist conclusions. Intentions remain for him never facts but interpretations, with the taint that this conveys for any specific claim of the Aghed as genocide and more generally, it seems, for any other genocide. (This implication would seem to extend to *any* action judged on the basis of an agent's intentions, but that broader claim need not be considered here.) Nichanian might have mentioned, although he does not, that the UN Convention specifically cites the intention to commit genocide as a necessary condition for the designation of an act *as* "genocide." (Among other implications here, this would exclude the possibility of an "accidental" genocide, although in principle, an unintentional or nonintentional act might produce the same outcome.)

There are, to be sure, intrinsic difficulties in judging intentions since they are never open to empirical inspection in the way that the acts allegedly based on them are. From that benign starting point, however, Nichanian lumps together interpretations that reach conclusions about intentions with all other interpretations (e.g., in the interpretation of a poem) as nonfactual. But in thus placing interpretation beyond the reach of facts, he is in effect stipulating a limit to that reach which conflicts basically with common usage and practice. One implication of Nichanian's position is that *any* judgment based on circumstantial (inferential) evidence is nonfactual; thus all charges of premeditated murder would be ruled "nonfactual" since they presuppose claims about the premeditation as a feature of that act and thus of any judgment made about it. The only authority for judgments on intentional acts in this account would then be social power—not evidence or truth. The common understanding that all inferential legal—and moral—judgments must and can have a basis on evidence—the facts of the matter—is assumed by him to be baseless.

The outcome of Nichanian's discussion is thus an extra- or transhistorical representation of the Aghed—beyond historical evidence and interpretation because counter-claims to any such representation are *always* possible. Such possibilities violate, in his view, the significance, in effect the self-evidence, of the Aghed, claiming thus a status of sacralization and uniqueness not only for it but presumably for any other "catastrophe" that (other) groups or persons find in their history; there seems no reason in fact to exclude from this transhistorical domain *any* act in which intentions figure. But even to remain only with genocide, there *have* been other genocides that share common, prima facie features with the Aghed; and also for them—contra Nichanian—the question of whether intentions impelled them is at once relevant and open to the test of evidence, at least as open as the identity of the groups victimized.

The impossibility in Nichanian's terms that any account of genocide as "genocide" could be measured by moral or legal—or historical—criteria seems arbitrary and in any event a high and unnecessary price to pay for recognizing *as facts* the atrocities committed against the Armenians with which Nichanian is mainly concerned. The implication that nothing is common among other events similar to the Aghed, nothing in their origins or outcomes, structures, or means that shapes the understanding of what occurred in them (for the purpose, for example, of taking preventative measures against future ones) goes beyond any evidence he provides. Yet that claim follows from Nichanian's account (is this also *its* intention?): a version of the Uniqueness Hypothesis, with uniqueness extended here to many Uniquenesses (applied specifically to instances of genocide). It is in these terms a historiographic irony that Lemkin's conceptualization of genocide was designed specifically to forestall such a conclusion as well as such events in the future, however diverse such acts would be in relation to their social or cultural sources and causes.

Larry May's critique of the concept of genocide is more systematically developed than Nichanian's, and as a consequence, is still more radical in its criticism. Whether one accepts his conclusions or not, he identifies central issues related to that concept, along the way providing a valuable checklist for reconsidering both genocide and "genocide." *But*—a very large "but"—an odd issue unsettles his critique, beginning with its implication that the phenomenon of genocide may not even be *possible*. This is not because of gaps in the received definition, but because May's "nominalist" premise repeatedly asserts that only individuals, not groups *really* exist. And what then, he asks his reader, happens to the "genos" in genocide? The nominalist presupposition here formally resembles Nichanian's assertion that "genocide is not a fact." Both statements have the status of stipulations; both are critical of the received view of genocide, rejecting methodological elements in it necessary for *any* historical analysis; and both present their own versions of the atrocity of "genocide" without, however, substantiating their central assumptions. May recognizes his own aporia: how can "genocide" be a credible concept if groups—the referent of "genocide" in the charge of group-murder as a crime—do not *"really"* exist?

May's nominalist premise here has a rich history. He cites Ockham and Hobbes as predecessors in arguing against theories of universals that had recurred in the philosophical world since Plato's critics had their say, and he could easily have included other canonical names. But he describes little of the historical or conceptual basis for this fundamental and lengthy debate, and his privileging of the one side here without considering the claims on behalf of its alternative is in effect to stipulate, not to argue. Yet—consistently or not—May raises substantive issues and proposals about genocide and "genocide" that warrant attention; why he would engage such issues, given his basic doubts about the standing of groups at all, is puzzling but is a question apart from what he says about "genocide" as he goes on to criticize it as if it *were* a possible or even a real crime.

One of May's criticisms of the concept of genocide can be quickly set aside as a straw man. This is his objection to assertions that genocide has been held to be the "worst of crimes"; against that assertion, he contends that certain other crimes are no less heinous. The claim he contests here has certainly figured, explicitly or tacitly, in much public discourse and in some legal findings as well (it lurks in the background of chapter 1 of this study and reappears as a flashpoint in the chapters to come)—and May's objection to it is certainly arguable. But it is important to note that neither the claim itself nor its history is intrinsic to the concept of genocide. The UN Convention on Genocide to which May repeatedly refers never cites genocide as "worse" than other crimes, let alone as the worst; the definition it attaches to "genocide" does not mention other crimes at all. Legal codes that mandate punishments for specific crimes do reflect the alleged severity of those crimes, but even when such references appear, they are not usually, certainly not necessarily, included in the crime's definition—and nothing at all is said in the Genocide Convention about what punishment should be mandated for those found guilty of the crime. *Is* genocide the worst of actual or possible crimes? Perhaps, perhaps not—and the preceding chapter has pointed to some of the difficulties in making any such assessment. But the Genocide Convention's concern is not with that issue at all—beyond its assumption that genocide is indeed a crime—but with the question of how genocide is *distinguishable* as a crime at all.

May's metaphysical nominalism, on the other hand, has substantive and crucial implications for the concept of genocide, and although at times he qualifies that commitment, it remains the key to his criticism of the concept of genocide, with his basic line of argument explicit: if groups don't in fact exist, allegations of group-murder must be factitious—and, according to him, groups *don't* exist, certainly not in the sense that individuals do. Indeed, his nominalist view of group-identity asserts that concept's reducibility to features of individuals, thus, for example, the nominalist view of "group-rights" that is immediately relevant to genocide finds them to be at most functions of individual rights. But May ignores the many arguments that have been given for group "reality" (and rights) without refuting or even contesting them; his conceptualization of a normative understanding of genocide and "genocide" appears then *as if* (a qualification he himself introduces) the reference of those terms—groups—were real. Groups, then, exist in a virtual space, but only sufficiently, it seems, to be subject to denial and in contrast to the analysis he provides for atrocities otherwise called "genocide," as that analysis is based on his own nominalist principles.

May's critique addresses four main problems in the received concept of genocide as group-murder, raising objections to the Convention's stipulations of (1) what groups are subject to or "eligible for" genocide and how is that to be decided; (2) what actions warrant the charge of genocide; (3) what form of intention (*mens rea*) is required by claims of the act of genocide, and how such intention is to be determined; and (4) what the justifiable or obligatory responses to genocide are.

The question of which groups were to count as possible victims of genocide was a contentious issue in the drafting of the UN Convention and has surfaced repeatedly since then. As pointed out earlier, the Convention itself settled on four groups: "national, ethnical, racial, and religious," and as chapter 1 notes, although the Convention does not itself give reasons for singling out those groups, discussions at the time of the Convention's drafting cited both the (superficially) involuntary character of membership in those groups and the fact that it was those groups that had predominantly been victims of alleged genocides previously. May quickly objects to the first of these two reasons, convincingly citing voluntary means to membership in them all except for race (he might well have included the latter, as biologists increasingly view that category too as a social construct, and one which is biologically problematic).

The most basic reason supporting the choice of the four groups named in the UN Convention, however, is explicitly rejected by May: their relative importance in shaping cultural and individual identities. For he explicitly denies not only intrinsic but even historical differences in the roles of different group structures, asserting that no particular groups are more important than any others. The argument thus builds: since group membership for all persons may draw on the full range of human possibilities, to privilege certain groups (as the UN Convention does) is in the end arbitrary. Essentially all groups are equal—more precisely, they are equally *in*essential. And since (this is a separate point) an indefinitely large number of groups is available to fill any empty cultural space (including those that might have been "made" empty—for example, by genocide), the disappearance of any particular source of group-identity hardly matters. May here is certainly not saying that individual and mass murder do not matter—only that there is no significant conceptual difference between either of them and what has been asserted as distinctive, and distinctively criminal, in *group*-murder. In all of them—in the last of the three as well as in the first two—the moral violation, hence also any legal violation based on it, is exclusively the murder of individuals as individuals.

This is a large, provocative, and putatively empirical claim—for which, however, May provides little evidence other than his stipulated denial of any significant role for group-identity. About his more specific objections, it should be noted that nothing in the UN Convention precludes the addition of other groups to the four named in it. Beyond that, although May's insistence that all groups are ontologically equal—and "unreal"—suggests that *he* could not consistently add to the list or to the dangers that might confront groups as such, he does in fact propose amendments to the Convention in the *types of acts* that should count as genocidal (e.g., "prohibiting the use of the language of the group in daily intercourse or in schools").

Such amendments, constructive in themselves, continue to be shadowed, however, by his assumption that all groups are equal in social significance (if so, why should the linguistic denigration of a culture be singled out?) and easily replaceable. Here, it seems, history should have a voice: why, as he implies, would it not be necessary for the Genocide Convention to anticipate potential genocides against members of bridge clubs, bicyclists, dentists or redheads, if it is to be consistent in protecting members of the privileged groups named in the Genocide Convention? But a premise of the Convention is that some group-structures have historically been more important in the lives of societies and their members than others, and that this is a prima facie reason for protecting *them*. Can or should other groups—or other features of the groups named—be added to the list? The case for such additions needs to be made—but insofar it could or should be, it would follow from applying a standard of measurement close to that used for the listing of the groups already named in the Convention—Ockham's razor would seem a useful instrument here against May's own nominalist commitments.

The second question about the specific character of genocidal actions is crucial, indeed unavoidable if such actions are to be distinguished from other types of murder, most relevantly from mass murder which may involve the killing of even more people than any act of genocide. May's reasoning here moves in two different but complementary directions. On one hand, since groups derive whatever moral standing they have from the individuals composing them, genocide is a wrong because it kills individuals who are incidentally group members. But if genocide has no intrinsic relation to the group-identity of those killed, then to represent it as a distinguishable crime is gratuitous. On the other hand, even if one ascribes a measure of reality to groups, with genocide then threatening the group structure, May's stipulations that no one group is more important than any other and that replacement groups are always available implies little loss in the destruction of any particular group-structure. No harm, no foul—and thus again: why single out genocide?

May pulls back from the latter implication in its full form by acknowledging that for *survivors* of a genocide (since genocide may be charged even if not all members of the group are destroyed), the erasure of their group-identity's source may be a "harm" not easily repaired. Also here, however, the harm suffered is the experience of individual survivors, not the destruction of the group-identity as such. Furthermore, even if the harm admitted is as extreme as what Claudia Card identifies as "social death," there would still be the likelihood, on May's account, of a readily available successor social life—viewing the availability of such a successor as if it were a spare part for a machine. (An implausible, morally problematic implication also seems to follow here: that if *all* members of a group were killed, the group-harm suffered would be less than if only some members were, since in the former case, no survivors would remain to suffer the loss of what the group-structure had given them; there would also be no need, so far as the survivors are concerned, to find for them a successor group as a replacement.)

What exactly *is* the harm that might be suffered by individuals who did survive a genocide? May comes close here to conceding that the harm caused would be a disrupted sense of identity as the surviving group members were cut off from their group's cultural norms—a wedge with potentially large consequences in his blanket criticism of the role of group-identity. For if individual identity is even minimally dependent on group relations, the latter would have a measure of reality that the individual alone does not. And *that* claim is the crux of views opposed to May's nominalism—holding in contrast that "the self" (any human self) is a social self, with the individual at least as dependent on the group as the group is on the individual. Indeed, if any premise underlies the UN Convention on Genocide, it is that the "murder" of a group-structure is both a purpose of genocide and a significant loss suffered when that purpose is realized. Genocide may, but *need not*, involve physical murder, a condition that May recognizes without admitting its implications. As has already been discussed, the Convention stipulates that genocide can be committed by the prevention of births within a group or by the forced assimilation of a group's children into other populations (Articles 2d and 2e of the Convention). The "harms" that the latter inflict are not to the living (in the first instance) but to potential future lives that are denied to the then vanished culture (in both instances)—basically, in the destruction of the group-identity as such, which is clearly the sticking point for May who is able to write: "It is very unclear what precisely the harm is when a group is lost. . . . With the loss of one group, it does not follow that there is even one less group in the world." The counterclaim to this contention requires elaboration, but May's account hardly recognizes that there is even an issue here.

This is not the context in which to present systematic arguments for the existence of the human self as essentially social or, contra May, for the reality of groups on the scale that such a claim would require. But sources of evidence for both of these are readily available, among them, as already cited, the institution of language which remains a powerful instance and condition of group creation and existence, irreducible to individual awareness (or "individual characteristics," as May calls them). In terms of group-rights, the right of national self-determination—like the right to existence violated by genocide—cannot be ascribed to or exercised by an individual. These are the sort of difficult issues facing metaphysical nominalism when it turns to analyzing the complex phenomenon of human culture and social structures.

For his third point, May addresses the issue of intention that is pivotal in Nichanian's critique, and does this more systematically and usefully than Nichanian. One of May's objections here is directed against the concept of collective intentions, on which the nominalist's unsurprising position is that the role of the collective in that concept is at most a metaphor or figure of speech for bundled or "shared" individual intentions: "Collectivities . . . are fictions." For individual intentions, May finds no similar difficulty, in effect endorsing the Genocide Convention's provision for individual responsibility once individual intention is determined, although the determination of individual intentions faces many of the same evidentiary problems as does any account of collective or corporate intentions. A knottier problem for May's account is the Convention's stipulation that genocidal intention would be directed against the group "as such," perhaps also as originating in a part or whole of a group "as such" that perpetrates the crime. May's reading here interprets the phrase "as such" to signify "some sort of vague discriminatory animus" motivating the crime. It would be difficult (with or without the phrase) to imagine the act of genocide in the absence of "some sort of animus," and it may well be that the Convention's reference to "as such" adds little to what it otherwise proposes in the way of intention. But a simpler and more direct explanation of the presence of that phrase would be to underscore the genocidal intention to destroy the group as *also* distinguishable from the attacks on its individual members who may or may not be intentionally murdered so far as concerns the act of genocide. This reading also conflicts, however, with May's view of the target of genocide as individuals who may or are likely to be incidentally members of any number of groups; thus again, we hear about the negligible loss incurred in the destruction of any one group.

May's analysis of the fourth point, bearing on justifiable and/or obligatory responses to genocide is the more important because that topic has so often been slighted in discussions of genocide and the UN Convention. An obvious reason for such silence is the reluctance of governments to accept an *obligation* to intervene in foreign affairs not involving their own citizens, and indeed May is himself more comfortable with justifiable than with obligatory intervention, citing the tradition of "just war" doctrine as a basis for the former but also, and more strongly, as a *difficult*, if on occasion necessary, condition. But justification, as May points out, does not entail obligation, and on that basis he stops short here, as he also does on the related question of what means of punishment or prevention would be entailed even if such an obligation were admitted. But the latter question—obligatory intervention by whom and how—is no less urgent than the other. Indeed, as communications in "real time" detail ongoing events definable as genocide with the possibility that intervention could impede or halt them, the urgency of a need for the means of intervention is intensified.

The UN Convention itself, ostensibly directed to the "prevention and punishment of genocide," does not specify any means of prevention other, implicitly, than what genocide's criminalization would do to that end, nor does it mandate specific punishments for those found guilty of the crime—and even the means for judging whether an act of genocide has been or is being committed are cited only in vaguely general terms. Punishment as a deterrent to crimes is itself known to have an uneven history; it is in any event no substitute for intervention at the time that a crime is being committed—which in the case of genocide understandably has been and undoubtedly will continue to be difficult to initiate. At the same time that May emphasizes the importance of intervention in an ongoing genocide—that is more important, he reasonably claims, than punishment—he also points to the practical difficulties of substantiating a charge of genocide while it is ongoing (also after the fact, but still more in the present tense). But this seems only to underscore the need for a provision in the Convention that would not only mandate intervention but add a mechanism for doing so that would provide an instrument enabling the United Nations to provide for intervention in time to halt or, even earlier, prevent a genocide's progress. This supplement to the Convention would obviously be compatible with May's analysis of the justification for intervention; it would also give weight beyond that to the Convention's assertion of a substantive basis for the charge of genocide—which May has been arguing against.

That these two accounts push back against what has served as a standard view of genocide is representative of certain elements in that reaction. May's study adds a useful systematic outline of issues confronting "genocide" and genocide if they are to remain a foundation for what has otherwise been recognized as an important legal, ethical, and historical norm. Nichanian's move toward what is at once a sacralization and rebuttal of genocide through the perplexities he finds in responses to the Armenian Aghed would leave that event (and other like ones) as transhistorical, beyond the reach of either explanation or verification. This has ample precedent in "uniqueness" claims as related to the Holocaust, for another example; the shared problems attending such claims are clear. Few advocates of that position, whether applied to a particular genocide or as a general view, regard historical analysis as *entirely* irrelevant to understanding the events at issue—and even that small opening suggests the possibility of a larger historiographic progression in which the temptation of sacralization loses much of its attraction. May's more sustained account assumes a methodological and metaphysical foundation which is debatable in ways he does not himself address, although at the same time he points to key questions requiring scrutiny in any substantive analysis of genocide and "genocide." The question "What is to be done?" thus persists both in and after these accounts, also leaving that question for the futures of both genocide and "genocide."

The Pushback and Its Search for a Replacement

The philosopher Paul Boghossian has been among the most outspoken critics of the Genocide Convention and, beyond that of the concept of genocide as such (the "such" as stated in the Convention itself—that is, as such). The specific objections he raises in "The Concept of Genocide" have varying force, but they do not in my view seriously challenge the importance of the Convention or its conceptualization of genocide. A number of basic issues are indeed unresolved in or around "genocide," and these have become increasingly visible in recent attempts to apply the charge of genocide in various international and national courts. Some of these longer-standing problems Boghossian addresses and finds insoluble; some he ignores in favor of straw men, which he then knocks over; and among others, he addresses recognized gaps in the UN Convention without acknowledging the various attempts that have been or might be made to remedy them. In still other parts of his criticism, he disputes the Convention's requirement of intention as a condition of genocide on grounds which, if generalized, would nullify important elements of virtually all contemporary civil and criminal legal codes. In arguing along these various lines, he provides a valuable systematic analysis of issues relevant to the Convention, although at the same time ignoring the fundamental accomplishment of the Convention itself, offering a minimal and finally misleading account of the motivation behind the concept of genocide as well as of its systematic structure. Group-murder becomes for him individual murder multiplied. In this, he does not go as far as we have noted the classical Draco does, by moving toward a one-size-fits-all conception of wrongdoing, but if any substantive proposal emerges from Boghossian's analysis, it is that the range of acts that have been and may be confronted under the heading of genocide would be addressed more comprehensively and precisely as individual murders (then treated additively by the number of victims). The time-tried concepts of "killing" or (more generally) "harming" are alleged by him to do everything that "genocide" does *and* to do this without that category's confusions or inflated rhetoric.

As earlier chapters here have shown, disputes about the Genocide Convention's definition of "genocide" are neither new nor startling. Many of the issues recently cited appeared in heated discussions when the Convention was drafted in or before 1948 and have persisted since: thus, for example, the central question about *which* groups should be recognized as "eligible" for genocide. Other issues have become clearer in the nearly seventy-year period since the Convention's adoption, most recently in the efforts of the International Criminal Court to apply judicially the charge of genocide. (It is worth repeating that "genocide" was included in the charge against defendants in the first Nuremberg trial in 1945, although it disappeared in the verdicts that came out of that.) Clearly, certain substantive problems remain in both the UN Convention and the very concept of genocide. But Boghossian's version and critique of those problems and his willingness simply to dismiss the category of genocide in its legal and moral standing call attention mainly to *symptoms* of the difficulties, not to their substance or sources; more importantly, it renders moot if it does not simply deny the possibility of amendments to the Convention that might resolve the issues cited in it but would also preserve its distinctive focus.

Consider, for example, one of Boghossian's objections mentioned previously in May's account: the claim that genocide has been viewed as "the most heinous of crimes." Against that, Boghossian, like May, argues that this assessment of genocide is problematic both in principle and in practice. Why Boghossian troubles with this matter might itself raise questions, since if genocide is not a distinctive or distinguishable crime as he later concludes, he need hardly quarrel with its popular ranking *among* crimes. But more substantively, true as it is that public discourse has at times cited genocide as extreme, even as most extreme among atrocities, Boghossian evidently means to direct his criticism against the *formal* conceptualization or definition of the term "genocide" as formulated in the Genocide Convention. This is a reasonable, even unavoidable focus, as the test of any putative legal concept would be to address its most authoritative formulation. But so far as that is his purpose, it is relevant to note that nowhere in the Convention (or in subsequent UN legislation on human rights) is genocide accorded priority over other atrocities or crimes. Certainly no claim to that effect figures in the term's *definition*, and so far as I can determine,

Raphael Lemkin himself never made such a claim about the atrocity he named and described.

The reasoning that led to Lemkin's articulation of the term and concept was much more restrained and nuanced in his claims about "genocide" in its legal as well as a moral formulation. In the 1930s, and thus before the "Final Solution" was initiated, Lemkin undertook to fill what he saw as the gap in international law that allowed governments— because of their sovereign "rights"—to do as they chose to groups within their national boundaries and to act in this way not only when the countries involved were at war with others but also during peacetime. This initial and then continuing concern for defenseless minorities eventually expanded to include groups and their members *across* national boundaries, but neither early nor late is there a claim by Lemkin or in the definition he proposed that genocide is the "most heinous" of crimes. Lemkin's initiative focused on the need for legislation to fill a gap in the international legal structure, advocating also that violations of the proposed legislation should be punished (in the future or even, as at Nuremberg, retroactively). Of course, genocide figured in these discussions as a *serious* crime, but how it was to be ranked relative to other serious crimes was not part of Lemkin's brief or of the Genocide Convention. If "genocide" is to be criticized analytically, then, and even if the question of comparative evil in relation to other atrocities warrants scrutiny independently, the two issues are not necessarily linked. (Even on the empirical finding that genocide has often in public discourse been cited as the most extreme or heinous of atrocities, it is also reasonable to ask what about the atrocity itself has conduced to that.)

Other, more substantive, issues do figure in Boghossian's critique—issues to which the concept of genocide has arguably been itself at least a partial response. So, for example, there is the contentious legal and moral question of the relation between quantity and quality in wrongdoing, outlined as an issue here in chapter 2. Is the premeditated murder of ten people more culpable than the premeditated murder of one? the murder of millions? the murder of specified groups rather than of indiscriminately attacked individuals? Do differences in judgment about these—as they occur—hinge on numbers alone? It is significant that, although the UN Convention specifies several distinct conditions as defining genocide, it makes no reference at all to numbers. Boghossian does not himself seem to regard counting as relevant except in the different, if related, context of the vagueness he alleges in the Convention's stipulation that genocide may be ascribed to acts directed against members of the groups attacked as wholes or "in part" (in Article 2 of the Convention).

In relation to that phrase and the associated question of numbers, Boghossian finds the vagueness so great as to amount to absurdity, since the "in part" qualification could presumably justify the charge of genocide for acts committed against even a *small* part of a group's membership (so long as the acts were committed against them because of that membership; see more about this stipulation below). And a further implication of this interpretation, as Boghossian points out, is that genocide could be committed not only against a small number of a group's members, but against the smallest number possible—that is, against *one* such member. Genocide, in other words, might be occasioned by an individual murder committed on the grounds that the victim is a member of the group that might be otherwise persecuted—or even, because of the importance attached to intention in the identification of genocide and the related fact that genocide need not be completed but only attempted, for the *attempted* murder of such a single person (provided, again, that the reason for the act or attempt is the person's membership in a specified group).

Now unless one assumes great carelessness or stupidity in the UN formulation and in Lemkin's own reasoning, the stipulation of "in part" would have been proposed as a possible aspect of genocide as crime, and that aspect indeed becomes clear in the record of discussions at the time of the UN formulation. From that record, the phrase "in part" was included to anticipate possible attacks against key members of a group (thus a part of the group) who would be essential by their positions or abilities for its survival. That role could be anticipated, thus providing a likely target for a genocidal attack. In this sense, the phrase represents a precaution consistent with the overall aim of the Convention—one that could be acknowledged even if one acknowledged at the same time the need (and possibility) of its more precise formulation.

Boghossian's objection here, furthermore, reflects itself a partial rendering of the concept of genocide, focusing on one condition of genocide (acting against individual persons because of their membership in a particular group) at the expense of another even more basic to the concept of genocide: its reference to the killing not of individuals but of the group (the "genos"). Again, recognition of this second condition does not mean that the destruction of a group may not involve the physical killing of individuals, only that it *need* not do this, even in part, since the destruction of a group can be accomplished also by other means, as the Convention stipulates: by the prevention of births within a group or by the forced assimilation of a group's members into another populace. The latter conditions are crucial for understanding the Convention precisely because they do *not* involve the physical murder of individuals; they make sense in context only when the purpose of designating genocide a crime is understood to construct protection for a group, not (primarily) for individuals.

Of course, the murder of individuals as a means of genocide is *relevant* to the Genocide Convention's broader intention. Such instances of genocide as the Turks' attacks on the Armenians in 1915–17 or the Nazis' "Final Solution," both of which caused millions of deaths and are cited by Boghossian, remain horrific paradigms. But these two instances are paradigmatic of genocide not only or, I have been arguing, primarily because of the mass murder of individuals but because they point more directly and explicitly to genocide, the murders of a group qua group, than other occurrences of genocide that preceded them, and certainly more than others that had been the result of genocidal actions that did not involve physical murder (as in mass sterilization or the forced integration of one group into another). The physical murder of members of a group because of their group-identity thus affects a "double murder," in Lemkin's own phrase: murder of the individuals *and* murder of the group—with the latter, however, being the distinctive feature of genocide. Charges of individual murder, even on a mass scale, do not envision or attempt this purpose or telos of genocide; hence the need, conceptually and practically, for distinguishing genocide, as act and idea.

Admittedly, this shift in emphasis from the victimization of individuals to the victimization of groups may seem only to defer the question of how or whether numbers enter into the concept of genocide. And clearly, to speak of "group-murder" would be vacuous unless one also identified the nature and size of groups to be subsumed under that rubric—assuming that *some* such criteria of inclusion and exclusion would be necessary. The question of how many members a qualifying group must have—or how many of them must be killed or threatened—is relevant but not necessarily more decisive and certainly not exclusive of other conditions for defining "genocide." Whether or not the murder of a single person could in the formal definition count as genocide, it seems clear that it could meet the definition's conditions if only the victim was killed as a member of the targeted group, because of that membership. But unless the group attacked has a membership of *only* one, this would not satisfy the still more basic requirement for genocide: that what distinguishes it from individual or mass murder is its purpose of destroying the group of which individuals harmed are members. From records available about the drafting of the Genocide Convention, it becomes clear that the purpose of including the "in part" words in the phrase stipulating that genocide could be directed against a group as "a whole or in part" was to forestall the killing or threat to the leadership or elite of a group. Such an act might in certain circumstances threaten the survival of the group, and this suggests that rather than speaking only of "part" of the group (leaving an opening in that limited context for Boghossian's "one-man" interpretation), this leadership "part" should be (and could be) further specified. (There would still be the difficulty of determining intention in relation to this part of the group, but no more difficulty formally than in defining the "group" either as a whole or in relation to its more broadly held intention.)

The questions persist, however, of how many people are required in order to constitute a group and what other qualifications would be necessary or relevant in determining a group's "eligibility" for genocide. The four groups cited in the UN Convention are named with no accompanying estimate of numbers, although the assumption is clear that they would usually be substantial: nation, ethnicity, race, religion. To be sure, instances of those groups have also varied widely in the numbers of their members, and there is no reason in principle why the number should not be very small (perhaps even, and also as a result of genocide, extending to the last and single person remaining). But the Convention's purpose is (I have argued, primarily) directed against the destruction of a group, and if the group's membership had been reduced to one, by whatever means, that would evidently be sufficient evidence. Could there be a group whose membership had never been more than one? But there seems no reason for contesting the terms of the Genocide Convention because of such an unlikelihood when the threat to significantly large groups has been not only possible but actual. This issue of numbers extends also to the number of victims—or their proportion within the specific group—required to justify a charge of genocide. (Even advocates for the Convention in the US Senate regarded this as an impediment to ratification when the Senate first considered that action in 1950.) But here consideration returns to the condition specified for genocide of "intent"—with the status of determining that, in individuals or corporately, *always* a matter of inference and not open to direct inspection or to formulation as an algorithm (although minimal numbers could always be adopted as conventions.)

Boghossian further objects to the Convention's list of groups eligible for genocide as arbitrary because of its exclusion of certain groups no less significant in shaping social identity than those named—like those reflecting economic, ideological, or class identity. These examples (and perhaps others), he claims, have at least claims no less strong than those named in the Convention. As already noted here, this objection was raised both in principle and with specific reference at the time of the drafting of the Genocide Convention, and although the decision to exclude certain of the groups not named might (and perhaps should) still be contested, two counterclaims challenge the argument that this is an *essential* feature (and defect) in the concept of genocide. The first counterclaim—that important social groups have been excluded—is not by itself inconsistent with the concept of genocide as stated; the fault here (so far as it is one) could be remedied simply by expanding the list of groups covered by the Convention as based on the concept of genocide itself. The Convention itself does not preclude the process of amendment; as consistent with UN and parliamentary procedure, such amendments would be procedurally possible.

The second objection to Boghossian's criticism of the specification of the four groups that the Convention names as eligible for genocide reflects his avoidance of any explanation of *why* the four groups named appear in the UN Convention at all. Admittedly, the Convention does not provide such an explanation, but one might nonetheless assume (as Boghossian himself does) that the choice of the groups designated was not arbitrary. Indeed, the explanation for inclusion of the groups on the UN list is crucial for understanding the intention of the Convention as a whole. Although the record of discussions at the time of the Convention's adoption is sketchy, it is sufficiently detailed to contest Boghossian's own explanation, which is limited to the underlying assumption he finds in the Convention that the four groups cited there were viewed by its drafters as natural kinds: "indelible." He then criticizes this alleged basis on the grounds both that there are other equally important "indelible" kinds (e.g., gender) that remain unmentioned *and* that the ones named are not in fact indelible. On this last point he cites the possibility of religious conversion, but he might have added the possibilities that citizenship can be given up or acquired, that the socially constructed status of race has effectively supplanted claims of its biological basis, and that voluntary assimilation to "ethnical" groups different from a person's original one has become a distinguishing feature of modernity.

And in fact, there is no reason to assume that Lemkin and the drafters of the UN Convention were so muddled or so eager to pass *something* in the way of legislation as an epilogue to World War II that they mistook these obvious features of the groups they included (and the others that they excluded), since the groups named are singled out because of their *perceived* roles quite apart from any intrinsic or essential qualities. Thus even if one assumes the mistaken understanding that Boghossian ascribes about the "indelibility" of the groups included, it is still more compelling that among the group-affiliations in the contemporary world with strong effects on individual identity or "self-making," these four groups, as conventionally defined and viewed, have been powerful forces. A demonstration of this by thought experiment would be by imagining the process of contemporary cultural and identity formation *in the absence* of any—still more, of all— those four modalities.

This minimalist justification for the four groups does not, furthermore, preclude adding other groups or subtracting one or another of those cited as their significance diminishes; nothing in the Genocide Convention stipulates exclusivity or permanence for the groups included. But it does provide a standard for subsequent nominations, both relevant and necessary because the number of possible groups that could be included is virtually limitless: bicycle riders, dentists, Phi Beta Kappas, persons over (or under) six feet tall, aunts, chess players, and so on. To be sure, there may be individuals for whom these or other "small" group-affiliations have indeed been central in shaping identities. But the standard met by the four groups is a function of their extent and depth; no fixed figures or degrees of intensity are given for those measurements—it is unlikely that there could be formulas for determining them—but this is not sufficient for denying significant differences between the groups included and the much greater number of those excluded.

Boghossian mentions the possibility that "group-rights" are somehow related to the concept of genocide but then drops that reference without elaboration. This omission is unfortunate since, complicated as issues surrounding theories of group-rights are, the claims for such rights bear on the questions that Boghossian himself raises. The Genocide Convention does not mention rights at all, individual *or* group. But it is reasonable to infer—from Lemkin's own comments elsewhere—that underlying the Convention's concept of genocide is a commitment to rights doctrine and, in that, also to group-rights. The tradition of "rights talk" prior to World War II focused on individual rights, a dominant emphasis from the origins of rights theory in Enlightenment political philosophy forward. But since the Holocaust and the subsequent conceptualization of genocide, group-rights have occupied a large space in the discourse about rights. Other factors than the Holocaust and the Genocide Convention contributed to this development, but the impact of those events on the recent attention to group-rights has been largely ignored—and both that omission and the relevance of that lineage is noteworthy. That association emerges as still another counter to Boghossian's dismissal of the relevance, conceptually as well as historically, of "genocide." For if groups can be said to have rights, surely for them no less than for individual persons the rights specifically bound to the rights bearer warrant attention. So, for example, the right to national self-determination, heralded in Wilson's Fourteen Points doctrine and reiterated after World War II in a number of United Nations declarations, *could* not be held by an individual person—and the same claim, still more basically, applies to genocide as violating the right of specified groups to their survival.

Admittedly these claims *assume* the existence of rights, as in a right to national self-determination (the nation here functioning as an instance of a group) or in the right of specified groups to avoid destruction; in that assumption, they sidestep systematic questions about the origin or ontological status of the rights they declare. But those same important questions apply to the derivation and status of *individual* rights no less than of group-rights, and the issues they involve require more extensive analysis than I can attempt here. There have been theories of politics and ethics which avoid rights talk entirely—at times explicitly rejecting it—most polemically in utilitarianism, but also in the naturalist Aristotelian tradition and "virtue" ethics. No less evident, however, have been the debates about the comparative advantages or disadvantages of rights theories, and whatever position one holds about those disagreements, it seems clear that political discourse that draws on rights theory has figured largely in its modern history—which is all that need be granted for the moment in emphasizing the role of group-rights in relation to the concept of genocide and vice versa.

Arguably, the key substantive issue raised by Boghossian involves the role of intention in the definition of genocide. That role affects the Convention's definition of genocide in two different ways. The first of them is as in the general condition that genocidal acts result from an "intent" to commit genocide in the several possible forms of its expression. In that broad context, the term's implication seems clear enough: there can be no "accidental" genocides or at least they will not be taken account of—and Boghossian raises no objection to that implication. (It is conceivable that a group and its members might be attacked or annihilated by chance—if someone accidentally presses the wrong button, for example—but that is unlikely enough to be ignored or at least reserved for another legal category.) The UN Convention does not specify genocide to be itself a group action or expressing a group intention, but it is as difficult to imagine that act as the work of a single person, as it is to think of its occurrence as simply accidental.

The second aspect of intention is, however, seriously flawed in Boghossian's view, and his objection surfaces in relation to the words "as such" in the Convention's Article 2: "Genocide means any of the following acts committed with intent to destroy, in whole or in part, a national, ethnical, racial or religious group as such." The last two words here—"as such"—are indeed puzzling, and one might, as Boghossian points out, read them as redundant, simply repeating that the intent is directed against the group and against its members because they are its members. Boghossian prefers a different reading, however, which has itself two aspects. The first is an understanding of the group "as such" to mean "just because it is that very group," where Boghossian takes "just" to mean "only" as though that were the single contributory factor or motive for the act of genocide. This is a plausible but not necessary reading, since an alternative possibility comes clear in the objections he himself directs against it when he argues that "It is nearly never the case that the *sole* explainer for why someone acts to kill or harm large numbers of people is *just* [again, this has been his own term] the identity of those people."

The latter claim certainly holds for the two instances of "genocide" that Boghossian accepts as primary examples, but it also points to a question about Boghossian's reading of the Convention. For nothing in the phrase "as such"—or for that matter, any place else in the Convention—precludes motives *in addition* to the "as such" condition insofar as it is taken to mean *at least* that the group and its members would be attacked for its identity. The Nazis attacked the Jews as a group, the babies and elderly among them together with others. But the ostensible justification for this was that the Jews as a group posed serious—potentially fatal—dangers to the German "race" and culture: that the Jews, as both capitalists and communists, as both inferior and superior sometimes in the same respects as a contagious disease, and as isolated or insular, had caused enormous damage to societies of which they had been part, as evidenced in the backstabbing role they played in Germany's defeat in World War I. And so on. That this "justification" had no foundation in fact would not affect or diminish the act of genocide ostensibly based on it (and other beliefs), nor would such refutation obstruct the charge of genocide directed against the Jews as a group "as such": against them individually because of their group-membership and against the group (also as such).

If one asks about the conditions for a finding of guilt in the premeditated murder of a single person, evidence must show deliberation and planning of the murder (and then the murder itself): the victim is intended as victim. Can there be additional contributory intentions? Of course. Who would deny a motivating place to such motives and then intentions as revenge, jealousy, avarice, lust, and so on? Do such factors which contribute to "the" intention to commit murder detract from the premeditated act as premeditated? Not at all. To be sure, even individual intentions cannot be inspected directly and thus are only to be inferred, and the difficulty of determining

the corporate intentions typically responsible for genocide is still more severe. But this is not a conclusive argument against the relevance of intentions or premeditation
in assessing either individual or corporate actions. Nor is
the supposed counterevidence that Boghossian cites,
in the cases of both the Turks and the Nazis, that neither of
their attacks was fully genocidal because they both made
room evidently for exceptions: the Turks in certain cases
resorting to expulsion rather than annihilation, the Nazis
allowing for escape in instances where they were bought
off by wealthy potential victims. Exceptions of this sort,
like exceptions to any generalization, would invariably—
and rightly—be weighed in the balance of evidence overall. It would surely be excessive to infer that because of
inconsistencies in relation to the "Final Solution" on the
part of some Nazis who could be bribed to ignore their
own supposed commitment to racial dangers by making
exceptions for "good" Jews, the actions of so many other
Nazis (often of themselves as well) should be dismissed.
The elaborate Nazi system of more than ten thousand
concentration camps and the six notorious "death camps"
would seem weightier evidence of purpose and implementation than the instances of finding a place for exceptions that occurred. What is clear from the history of the
"Final Solution" is that the plan emerged over time and
with economic, geopolitical, nationalist motives in addition to racial and antisemitic ones, and that even the latter
motivation represented a bundling of reasons. That such
a variety converged on the intention to commit genocide does not erase or even dilute what turns out then to
be the primary goal of the intention itself: genocide against
the Jews, the group, and *as such.*

Questions can be raised about the usefulness or precision and thus justification for virtually any legal or moral formulation. Should manslaughter be distinguished from murder? Both involve culpability and the victims in both cases are dead. Is there a point to measuring *degrees* of murder? If so, what algorithm can be used for determining which degree applies in any particular case? Is there more than a nominal distinction between killing and murder? (The sixth of the Ten Commandments is sometimes translated from the Hebrew root ["retzach"] as prohibiting the one, sometimes the other—arguably reflecting more than simply linguistic ambiguity.) And so on. In this sense, difficulties in the definition of "genocide" and then in ascertaining when the phenomenon has occurred are common in jurisprudence and moral evaluation—but they are not by that fact found sufficient for rejecting the concept or altering its status as designating a crime.

The crucial question remains whether the concept of genocide points to an act sufficiently different from crimes resembling but not identical to it to warrant a criminal category of its own. "Mass murder" is a conventional and indeterminate rather than a legal term, in contrast to "genocide" which specifies a type of murder within that broader category where other important distinctions already exist, as between murder and manslaughter, together with degrees of each. "Crimes against humanity" which has a juridical history and life of its own (although, as a technical designation, not a long one) is a category that thinkers about human rights like William Schabas have proposed as a replacement for "genocide" on the grounds that it avoids the vagaries found in "genocide" yet covers any actions to which that (in his view, vague) concept might be applied.

Commenting on Boghossian's critical essay, Schabas agrees in large measure with Boghossian's objections to "genocide," extending that criticism with a proposal to replace "genocide" as a criminal category by "crimes against humanity." The latter, Schabas claims, would cover whatever crime the former points to and do so without facing the problems that "genocide" poses. Schabas himself in his earlier study of both genocide and "genocide" had distinguished between what he called "primary examples" of genocide directed against the Jews, the Tutsis, and the Armenians, and other marginal or even failed "examples," emphasizing that "genocide" was clearly applicable to at least those three primary collective atrocities. It is unclear why he later backtracked on that claim, although it is evident that this newer option of "crimes against humanity" is *also* meant to include what had been known as "genocide." On examination, however, the category, "crimes against humanity" can be shown to exhibit many of the faults that Boghossian and Schabas find in "genocide" with the *additional* liability of obscuring the particular violation on which the concept of genocide focuses. "Crimes against humanity" is unmistakably (no doubt deliberately) a portmanteau phrase; the open-ended efforts to name the violations it covers and what they have in common demonstrate this. A formulation about "crimes against humanity" with perhaps the strongest current standing is found in the Rome Statute establishing the International Criminal Court, drafted in 1998 and naming the charges to be addressed by the Court. It is significant that among the four crimes that the Court is charged with judging, "genocide" is referred to separately from "crimes against humanity" (also from

103

the two additional types of crime included: "war crimes" and "the crime of aggression"). This is a strong indication that at least for drafters and signatories of the Rome Statute, "genocide" would not be adequately addressed by the rubric of "crimes against humanity," whether because it is outside the latter's purview or because even if it were covered there, the act itself is sufficiently radical to warrant its independent characterization. (To be sure, certain atrocities would clearly qualify as transgressions in all four of the categories named.)

It is notable that among the eleven distinguishable crimes it does subsume under its category of "*crimes against humanity*," the Rome Statute does not mention genocide. That list of crimes begins with murder and extermination, then cites acts of enslavement, deportation of populations, imprisonment, torture, rape and sexual slavery, enforced disappearance of persons, apartheid, and finally the "persecution against any identifiable group or collectivity on political, racial, national, ethnic, cultural, religious, gender or other grounds that are regarded as impermissible under international law." This last reference is sufficiently broad to include the crime of genocide—but the decision to use the term "persecution" here also avoids naming that specific crime. This is quickly remedied in the same context, however, as "genocide" and *its* form of murder is identified as still a different one of the four crimes that the International Criminal Court is charged with prosecuting. The groups named here as subject to the "persecution" among "crimes against humanity" are more extensive than the four named in the Genocide Convention; the charge to the ICC includes as subject to such crimes political, cultural, and gender groups as well as "other groups regarded as impermissible under international law" (question-begging as a category, although also with a possible reference to the Genocide Convention as among other sources of "international law.")

Because no limitations are intrinsic to the Genocide Convention, there is no incompatibility between the eligible groups cited in the Convention and those added in this passage of the Rome Statute. At the same time, however, the problems that "crimes against humanity" is meant to overcome seem in fact only to rehearse problems that Boghossian and to some extent Schabas attribute to "genocide." Thus the phrasing as cited of "persecution of any identifiable group or collectivity" leaves open the question of who is authorized to do the "identifying" and on what grounds or in relation to what numbers: these remain problems raised about—and contested in—the original formulation of "genocide." Another significant issue appears in relation to "crimes against humanity" as applied to all the violations under its charge: that the acts specified are "committed as part of a widespread or systematic attack directed against any civilian population *with knowledge of the attack*" (emphasis added). The "knower" here presumably refers to the attacker's awareness, and the attacker's "knowledge" is but another way of referring to an intention, if only by implication and thus at least as based on circumstantial evidence. (Whether such "knowledge" includes recognition of the wrongfulness of the act would be a separate question.) Here too, then, the problems criticized in the concept of genocide resurface in only slightly different guise, underscoring the objection that I would emphasize to the reformulation—that it faces the same difficulties that it is intended to overcome or sidestep in "genocide" itself.

Chapter 4

One final but overriding issue in relation to the concept of "crimes against humanity" as the Rome Statute defines them and as that concept is proposed as a replacement for "genocide" comes up explicitly in relation to what I have been claiming is the crux of the Genocide Convention: that it defines the crime of genocide as directed against groups, not against individuals except as they are involved in the groups intended for extermination. And "crimes against humanity," when it cites as culpable only the "persecution" of the groups named, stops short of recognizing the goal of their extermination as distinct from forms of persecution for which that it is *not* a goal. The conflation here of all forms of persecution obscures the distinctiveness of group-murder, which the Genocide Convention addresses squarely, and although there is no doubt that acts of "genocide" would be "covered" by "crimes against humanity," the distinctiveness of that form of persecution is lost in this proposed revision. Racial segregation is obviously an instance of persecution, but it is nonetheless different from individual murder and still more different from genocide, however it may figure as a preface to either. Could the category of "crimes against humanity" be revised to include the specific act of group-murder? Of course. But then the search would begin all over again for answers to the same questions and issues that have surfaced in objections to the original definition and conceptualization of "genocide." It would be a search, in other words, for what has already been articulated, with all its gaps and vagaries, in the UN Convention on the Punishment and Prevention of the Crime of Genocide.

Part II

Genocide as Past and Presence

"Genocide" and "Holocaust"

Language as History

The links and disconnects between the terms "genocide" and "Holocaust" are intriguing for the issues they raise about linguistic representation, with specific implications for the popular currency of those terms as well as for their roles in historical writing and discourse. The chronology of the relation between the terms is itself worth noting, with "genocide" the earlier of the two, although not by much, and as it was itself subsequently influenced by details of the events gradually assembled under the heading of "the Holocaust." The term "genocide" first appeared in print in Raphael Lemkin's *Axis Rule in Occupied Europe*, and although his intense concern with genocide preceded the Nazis' "Final Solution," that policy and its implementation which took the lives of forty-nine members of his own family had an understandably strong effect on him. That he, in his efforts on behalf of genocide legislation, thought it necessary to downplay this great personal interest because of what he believed to be its general significance only added to the intensity of those efforts.

Chapter 5

Already in the 1930s, Lemkin, then a young rising jurist in Warsaw, had noted with increasing concern that minority groups, wherever they were, had virtually no protection under international law. (He was also during this period an early advocate for support in the home for working mothers as still another "minority" group.) In the international legal structure, policies or regulations and the acts based on them formulated according to the law within a recognized state were considered to be only that country's business; no other nation or international body had the authority to interfere with them, irrespective of the home country's policies or the procedures by which they had been formulated or applied. Since, furthermore, a crucial test of relationships between countries occurred in times of conflict or war, the common appeal to a "fog of war" defense for apparent crimes against vulnerable groups often overrode whatever other protective mechanisms might have been invoked, such as the several Geneva Conventions dating back to the nineteenth century (of which not even all the European nations were signatories).

Early in World War II, after the Germans invaded first Poland and then Russia, Winston Churchill in a radio broadcast on August 24, 1941 tellingly described the Nazis' actions against civilians in these countries as "a crime that has no name." It was Lemkin who soon afterward gave that crime a name, identifying in "genocide" the act of murder committed against individual persons solely because of their identity as members of a group and with the still more basic intent of destroying the group: thus "genocide," parallel and yet distinct from "homicide" with its specification only of an individual victim or victims.

In 1945, Lemkin, who was present at the Nuremberg trials, urged the Allied judges of that International Military
Tribunal to try the Nazi officials on grounds of the genocide for which the Nazi regime had been responsible. And
"genocide" was indeed included in the indictment issued
at the first of those trials although it was subsequently
omitted in formulations of the convictions finally arrived
at; the charges for which the Nazi officials were convicted
in that first trial specified "crimes against humanity," "war
crimes," and "crimes against peace" but not "genocide."
After this frustrated effort, Lemkin shifted his attention to the nascent United Nations where, walking its
halls in Lake Success, New York, and cornering heads
of state, ambassadors, and delegates in the effort to persuade them, he built on long-standing grievances especially of such small countries as Ethiopia, Ecuador, and
the Philippines, to gather support for the votes required
to pass what the UN General Assembly in December 1948
adopted as the Convention on the Prevention and Punishment of the Crime of Genocide. Because that resolution
by the General Assembly required individual ratification
by the legislatures of at least twenty (of the then fifty-two
UN member states), Lemkin spent much of the next two
years attempting to win those necessary votes—skillfully
drawing here too on the individual histories and grievances of a broad range of countries. Thus he managed in
the midst of the conflict affecting the newly independent
Israel to win ratification of the Convention by the legislatures of Jordan and Saudi Arabia as well as by that of
Israel. (It would be forty years later, in 1988 and after having previously rejected ratification four times, that the US
Senate finally voted to ratify the Convention.)

Lemkin's own life after the formal ratification of the UN Convention brought it into effect centered on urging its implementation and enforcement, as well as on efforts to persuade additional governments to ratify it. The need to protect minority and group populations, which for Lemkin had begun as a young lawyer in Poland (according to his autobiography, even before his university years, as he read about persecutions prior to and during World War I), persisted for him from then on and virtually to the point of obsession. It is likely that he could not have accomplished what he did without that single-mindedness, but it also exacted a cost in both his personal and professional life as he came to alienate even individuals and groups who had been his supporters but differed from him about tactics and strategies. When he died in 1959, the man who had been meeting not long before that with leading statesmen of the world and had been nominated for the Nobel Peace Prize was living alone in a rented room largely paid for by gifts or "loans" from others; his burial in a Queens cemetery was attended by seven people and was also paid for by a contribution. Lemkin's own end was, however, only the beginning of the story of genocide, which survives now as "genocide": his conceptual and practical monument. It also converges with "the Holocaust" and the origins and connotations of *that* phrase.

Years passed after World War II—and after the adoption of the Genocide Convention—before the complicated and far-flung details of "the Holocaust" could be fully understood as a single corporate event, the parts of which were directed by an genocidal intention against the Jews; that intention, if not the exclusive among the goals of the Nazi leadership, certainly figured as an important one. In reflecting on the evolution of "the Holocaust" linguistically and conceptually as well as in its immediate consequences, it seems clear that the Holocaust itself virtually never appeared to its victims as the totalizing genocide that would retrospectively identify it. In the face of their individual and group's suffering, few of the Jewish millions were in a position to recognize the broad and intricate extent of the atrocity that was claiming them individually. Lemkin himself, even after he coined the term "genocide" and found himself and forty-nine members of his family victims of the Nazis, could have had only a limited grasp of the complicated development of the "Final Solution" as implemented. (Unlike most early readers of Hitler's *Mein Kampf*, Lemkin during the early 1930s saw in it and took seriously the *intent* for genocide, but its *means* were still to be articulated.)

When the concentration and death camps in eastern Europe were overrun and liberated by Allied forces in 1944 and 1945, the survivors were typically mentioned in news accounts (as in the *New York Times*) as "slaves"— suggesting principally that they had been subjected to a harsh form of forced labor. Part of the difficulty for such accounts reflected a more general gap between the limits of language in relation to the Nazi systematic plan of extermination. It is not only that "genocide" had to be coined for the overall act, but that other terms were also missing—some are still lacking—for certain of its more specific aspects. These include, for example, an adequate term even for the people deported to and held in the concentration and death camps. To call them "slaves" implies a relationship of coercion, but it also implies a primary function of labor of some kind. But that was at most true only provisionally and only for a small proportion of those in the camps. "Prisoner" or the German "Häftling" (used by the German administration) suggests a measure of security as well as a defined sentence—neither of which applied to the Jews. The designation of "Ka-tzetnik," after the "K" and the "Z" from "Konzentrazionslager," come close to adequacy as an ad hoc term based on the German, but would be misplaced if applied as a term to victims of genocides in general: the camps were integral to a specific structure and are not a feature of genocides as such. (Other putatively general terms raise similar difficulties; so, for example, the ill-defined label of the "Muselmann" ["Muslim"] applied in some of the camps, and with analogues in others, to those in the camps who had given up the will to live: Primo Levi's "submerged" ["sommersi"].)

Disagreements will undoubtedly persist about the first or defining application of the comprehensive term, "the Holocaust"; such disagreements include the question of who was responsible for the phrase's introduction and how it gained currency. It was in any event only in 1960, fifteen years after the war's end, that the annual index of the *New York Times* included an entry for "Holocaust" as referring to the Nazi genocide (the term "genocide" itself first appeared in the Oxford English Dictionary in 1955). The term "Holocaust" had surfaced in the intervening years, but the emerging recognition of a single and coordinated corporate act was crucial for identifying the Nazis' attempt to annihilate the Jews: a corporate act against a collective people. That recognition and its articulation took time for practical, conceptual, and linguistic reasons. Recognition of the myriad individual events up "the Holocaust" as related to each other and with a common intentional source was the decisive conceptual step here, requiring the assembly of accounts of the process that is still ongoing in evidence of understanding that event as a unified occurrence. The fact that in the end the Nazis failed to achieve their goal of annihilation is understandably obscured by the enormity of their intention and what they did toward realizing that goal. But beyond, even aside from, its historical and human enormity, that failure also remains significant for understanding the charge of "genocide" as it applied to "the Holocaust." In contrast to the accepted distinction between "murder" and "attempted murder," "genocide" need not on the Genocide Convention's definition be completed to qualify as "genocide." Evidence only of the intent or attempt by itself is sufficient, although that evidence would obviously require a basis in actions taken, not only (or for that matter, even necessarily) statements of intent.

Enough has been written about the phrase "the Holocaust" to warrant only a brief account here. "Holocaust" itself derives from the Septuagint translation into Greek of the Hebrew "olah"—a form of sacrifice at the Temple in Jerusalem in which the sacrificial offering is entirely consumed by burning, in contrast to offerings that were not entirely burnt or burnt at all. Derived from the Greek, "holocaust" would subsequently appear in English of the fifteenth and sixteenth centuries, by metaphoric transfer referring to total or extreme destruction, at first destruction by fire but then by any means—the latter as used by Milton, for example, in *Samson Agonistes*. (That the Greek had this influence, not the original Hebrew "olah," reflects the more common absorption in English of the Greek.) The word "holocaust," referring to great destruction or devastation, has since then appeared in common usage—for one notable more recent example, in Scott Fitzgerald's *The Great Gatsby* (1925) in which the novel moves toward its conclusion with Gatsby's murder and then his murderer's suicide. Fitzgerald concludes his description of that scene—Gatsby's body is found floating on the water of his pool—with the simple wording, "and the holocaust was complete."

Alternatives to "Holocaust" in reference to the Nazi genocide have been the biblical Hebrew term "Shoah" ("destruction," "catastrophe") which has come to be used more often in non–Anglo European languages, and the Yiddish-Hebrew term "Churban" (also "destruction"), applied traditionally to the destruction of the two Temples in Jerusalem. The use of these terms, together with variations on the "Nazi genocide" stem in part from reactions against the religious associations of "Holocaust" that might be understood to represent the Jewish victims as themselves "sacrifices." All the terms or phrases designate the event from the perspective of the victims, distinguished in this from the coded euphemism of the Nazis' "Final Solution" which represents the viewpoint of the perpetrators and appears in the coded German of the Nazis without the scare quotes. The code at work in that phrase—part of the systematic elaboration of a language of concealment where, for another example, "Sonderbehandlung" or "special handling" substitutes for "execution"—proposes as "final" and thus the most desirable "solution" to the "Jewish Question." Variations on "genocide" provide a neutral designation for the event in terms of perspective (from the point of view of the Germans as well, for whom the genocide of the Jews was regarded as justifiable). This would be more simply, "The Nazi Genocide of (or against) the Jews": a description of the act endorsed by Nazi leaders and then suffered by the Jews.

Still another linguistic or more precisely grammatical feature of "the Holocaust" warrants consideration in the phrase's use of the definite article, "the." At times, although less commonly, also that word appears in uppercase; more usual is its lowercase appearance together with "Holocaust," the first letter of which *is* in uppercase. This combination has substantive as well as linguistic consequences, principally the implication of uniqueness that has been often, although not necessarily associated with "the Holocaust": what it is that makes it a proper noun, with the "the" at the very least implying distinctiveness? A parallel appears in current references to "the White House." There are many white houses in Washington, DC and many more elsewhere, but to speak of "the White House," with the "W" and the "H" in uppercase points to a one and only. Admittedly, this association would occur only to those familiar with American political or social idiom—but for them at least, "the White House" has only the one possible reference. And the same force accompanies the phrase "the Holocaust," with its implication that of many possible holocausts, this one warrants the definite article and the upper case letter, "H": one out of all past or possible ones.

There have been many and repeated attempts to explain as well as to defend what allegedly *makes* the Holocaust "unique" as this usage suggests, with its implication of an event not only unprecedented but impossible to duplicate. There is irony in the fact that the claim often accompanying this usage adds that the Holocaust in addition to being unique is also "ineffable," "unspeakable," "incomprehensible," "beyond words"—terms or phrases that otherwise may appear with strongly positive connotations (as "beautiful beyond words" for a painting). The events or qualities thus designated do not necessarily imply a common quality of uniqueness, but that is often explicitly asserted in association with "the Holocaust," with its implication that no other historical event has had or could claim likeness to it. This claim was put most forthrightly in Yehuda Bauer's onetime contention that "Holocaust" should be considered as more than only a proper noun; that it not only marked a singular event but defined a category of which it was and would remain the only member—truly unique. Bauer subsequently modified this view, although other commentators have held to variations of it. (We have seen in chapter 4 examples of similar claims of uniqueness made in the context of other genocides: the Armenian phrase, "the Aghed" ["the Catastrophe"] in relation to the Turkish atrocities in 1915–17; for the Palestinian Arab population in prestate Israel, "the Naqba" [also "the Catastrophe"] marking the Arab armies' defeat in 1948 and the related expulsion of many of their inhabitants from towns and villages in the nascent state.)

There are, to be sure, differences among the events cited in these terms, but certain general comments can be made about the common claim in them of "uniqueness." That term by itself is neither more descriptive nor explanatory than "parallel" would be: a line is parallel only in relation to something else, typically another line, and so too, for claims of uniqueness. Uniqueness—the question is unavoidable—in relation to *what?* The differing accounts that have emerged of what exactly was unique in the Holocaust might well provide a background to questioning the claim itself. Other assertions of uniqueness, many of them commonplace, have no such problems: snowflakes are said to be unique in shape, and fingerprints are allegedly unique in the shapes of their lined patterns— "unique" in both cases implying neither identical precedents nor successors. Those unique features may support practical applications for the two instances, but there is no particular *moral* weight associated with that uniqueness: snowflakes and fingerprints remain just that and no more. Furthermore, there is a sense—virtually a tautology—in which claims of uniqueness can be made for *every* historical event: given the specific time and place of an occurrence, no *other* one exactly like it had previously occurred or will subsequently occur—that is, in exactly the same place at the same time. And again, the claims of uniqueness for the individual atrocities cited above (as well as others), although not inconsistent with one other—that any one of them is unique has no bearing on whether others might *also* be unique—suggests prima facie a need for qualifying the claims.

Furthermore, the core of the Holocaust as an historical event, unavoidable for any account of it, is the intention on the part of the Nazis to destroy the Jews as a group and as such. Not to convert or to integrate or to expel its members, but to "disappear" them individually and, still more pivotally, the whole of which they individually are part. That the "Final Solution" would take place before the eyes of the world, deploying instruments of selective yet mass killing; that the country primarily responsible for it had a notable cultural history—these aspects matter, reinforcing the claim that they do distinguish the Holocaust from other (prior) genocides. But also that acknowledgement does not shift the distinctive goal of that genocide from its center in group-murder itself. The accidental features on its periphery could not have the weight they have without that; to imagine the "Final Solution" *without* the purpose of genocide obscures the whole. The vicious Nazi rhetoric—the Jews as a cancer, as sub-human—might still have appeared and individual atrocities might still have occurred (many had occurred elsewhere and earlier in pogroms, but, however devastating, they were not then acts of genocide), but if only they had occurred, the weight of "the Holocaust" would have been largely nullified.

This returns us, then, to the term and concept of "genocide" and again to Lemkin who found widespread precedents of genocide—from the Assyrians to the Mongols, in the Hebrew Bible and in Greek and Roman history. To be sure, the concept in Lemkin's definition and applications is a broad instrument, unavoidably vague— and some allegations of genocide, including some of Lemkin's own, can be contested with good reason. Beyond that, in certain current uses, the term has become in effect a synonym for any extreme atrocity, and although common usage cannot be dictated, this attenuated use has the effect of blunting the specific distinction that "genocide" was intended to make. In any event, the term and concept are not responsible for their misuse; the more important question remains whether the primary and intended use of "genocide" is coherent and applicable. That it meets these requirements—as at the historical junctures cited—is the claim made here repeatedly and from a variety of angles, and to which the linguistic representation and detail of "genocide" comes in response. I hope that it has also been made clear that certain additions or emendations may be warranted in the recognized formulation of "genocide" in the Genocide Convention, but also that these can be introduced without altering the decisive point of the Convention in its conceptualization of the specific act of group-murder as a crime. It is this focus that "genocide" brings into full view—and unless any proposed replacement for it includes that focus and the force impelling it, there would still have to be room within it for "genocide" in its essential detail.

Chapter 6

Raphael Lemkin, Unsung Hero

Reparation

The enormity of the Holocaust makes it awkward, even unseemly, to speak about individual heroes who figured in it. Even individual *demonic* figures who have been singled out pale in comparison to the scale of the event they imagined and implemented. The sheer expanse of the Holocaust outweighs such references—its widespread, startling reach initiated by a civilized country in the midst of civilized Europe and, still more specifically, because it was a *genocide*, the murder of one group of people by another group, with the collective victims and perpetrators leaving individuals on both those sides almost beside the point. It was, after all, a *group* atrocity, for both its perpetrators and its victims: collectively imposed, collectively suffered.

To be sure, individuals on the two sides can be singled out for their singular roles—individuals among the Nazis and their collaborators who bore fuller, more direct responsibility than others for Nazi policies and actions. But also for them, without the millions of passive supporters and of indifferent bystanders, those directly responsible could not have done what they did. And then too, at the opposite extreme, were those individuals who rose above even the harsh test of even passive resistance, risking their lives to save others in disregard of what they or anyone were reasonably obligated to do. The phrase "heroic rescuers" or "righteous among the nations" (less palatably, "righteous Gentiles") has been applied to non-Jews who, without being under immediate threat themselves, came to the aid of persecuted Jews, in the process risking and at times losing their own lives. A number of them (approximately thirty thousand) have been recognized by individual name in the Yad Vashem memorial—undoubtedly others should be cited who are not—but again, here too, and severe though the judgment seems, the sheer magnitude of the Nazi genocide overpowers nobility even of this order.

Significantly, no analogous category has been proposed of "righteous" or "heroic" Jews, and also for this there is a reason, since the six million dead, however their fate reached them (many of them distant from personal Jewish identity, "half" or "quarter" Jewish and some fully assimilated culturally), had nonetheless paid with their lives for the pseudobiological identification imposed by the Nazis. Not heroism on that side either, then, although at least sufficiency as a collective fact. And this extends even to individual figures who *might* be singled out: Abba Kovner, the twenty-year-old partisan leader in Vilna, among the few who as early as 1941 and *within* the Holocaust foresaw its eventual extent; Hannah Senesh, the young Hungarian woman who had escaped to then Palestine and volunteered to parachute back into Hungary as a partisan where she was captured and killed; at least some members of the Jewish councils (the Judenräte), like Adam Czerniakow, the head of the Warsaw council, who, when confronted by the Nazi order to select Ghetto Jews for deportation to the camps, found suicide the one means to innocence. These and others among the partisans or resistance fighters in the ghettoes and the camps, heroic as they were in the standard terms of heroism, also remain lone, small-scale figures when viewed beside the massive symbolic number of "the six million."

So, why then continue writing here about Raphael Lemkin as a hero of the Holocaust, who indeed *was* Jewish; who, although having lost forty-nine members of his own family, himself survived the Nazi genocide mainly in the relative safety of the United States; who resisted not with arms but with words (with risk to his own health); but who yet should in my view be recognized as a hero, notwithstanding his relative neglect in the more than half century since his death (also *in* his death)? This neglect is itself fading, as Lemkin receives increasing attention; current work on at least three full-scale biographies of him has come to my attention. Yet the fact of the neglect remains, and the reasons for it, though necessarily speculative, reflect on the man himself. One such reason has undoubtedly been that in considering heroism, especially in the context of violence on the scale of the Holocaust, it has been common to focus on physical acts and their risks—and still more importantly on accomplishments during the lifetime of the person rather than on anything in the way of a bequest that the person might have left for the future. It is in any event against such considerations that I think it imperative, morally and culturally, to recognize our inheritance from Raphael Lemkin (the "our" here a human "our"), as his legacy still, seventy years after the

Holocaust ended and more than sixty years after his own death, remains very much (and even increasingly) present: significant in international law, in moral and political theory, in everyday discourse. The term (often the charge of) "genocide" appears in newspaper headlines and accounts with unfortunate regularity; terrible as the occasions of those references are, we remain indebted, for the word and the concept and so also for charges for which they are the foundation, to Lemkin more than to any other single person as the one who articulated what has become a central distinction in political, legal, and even commonplace thinking, with ramifications that extend even beyond what he himself anticipated.

The starting point of this bequest in systematic terms came with the conceptualization and naming of the crime of genocide: the focus of earlier parts of the present discussion, of a crime that in Lemkin's view had had a lengthy history without being recognized as such. The term "genocide" came to him after certain false starts with others (mainly, and even in 1933 with the Nazi threat dawning, "barbarity" and also, more restrictively in relation to cultural destruction, "vandalism"). "Genocide" itself did not have a ready reception, including criticism of its hybrid linguistic origin (the Greek "genos" and the Latin "cide"; was the criticism itself a gesture against racial mingling?). To that objection, however, Lemkin himself offered a witty one-word rebuttal: "bicycle"—the Latin "bi" and the Greek "kyklos [circle]" traveling comfortably together. Although coining a term that succeeds in entering the language is an accomplishment, it is not so rare or, often, important enough to mark a distinctive occasion. But that disclaimer does not apply to the term and concept of "genocide," since Lemkin identified by them a historical occurrence that, beyond its name, had not been recognized in its distinctive legal, political, ethical, or cultural character. The lack of a name had not *prevented* earlier acts of genocide (the analogy with diseases which pass as parts of others until they are discovered as individual and named is an analogue here), but the Nazi genocide had an explicitness in scope and deliberation that would have made it distinctive even if it had not been initiated in a supposedly civilized country in civilized Europe at a time when mass communications made its occurrence, despite the Nazis' efforts to conceal it, a matter of public knowledge. Lemkin's deep interest in the phenomenon of genocide preceded the "Final Solution," but that attack obviously crystallized the term and concept for him. In its extreme version, he emphasized, genocide—in contrast to massacres and mass murder—involved a "double murder" (his words): the individual victims but also, and prior to the individuals, the group of which they were members.

It was this type of act that Lemkin anticipated before World War II and then took as a challenge for the rest of his life—a crime which before that had escaped the reach of international law. The document that remains a monument to Lemkin's ideas and labor is the United Nations Convention on the Prevention and Punishment of the Crime of Genocide—still, since its adoption in 1948, the authoritative formulation of genocide: unchanged, unamended. Lemkin was himself directly involved in both the drafting, passage, and ratification of that document. He was present earlier, during the first Nuremberg trial of Nazis that began in 1945, exerting efforts there to have the crime of genocide included in the indictments of the

Nazis on trial and for which those found guilty would be punished. The term "genocide" did appear in the indictment leading up to that first, principal trial, but not in the ultimate findings of guilt that were reached; those were instead based variously on the concepts of "crimes against humanity," "war crimes," and "crimes against peace"— none of which, in Lemkin's view, adequately identified the crime of genocide.

Lemkin's path that brought him to the United Nations in 1948 was circuitous. Soon after the German invasion of Poland on September 1, 1941, Lemkin visited his parents who lived in the eastern Polish city of Wolkowysk, close to the farm and village Bezwodne of his earliest years; they refused to accompany him in the escape he planned, one that would take him from Poland through Lithuania and Latvia to Sweden, thence to Japan by way of Russia and finally—all this by April 1941—to the United States. There, through the intervention of acquaintances and friends made in the course of his work in international law, he had a temporary appointment at Duke University and shortly after that as chief consultant to the Board of Economic Warfare in Washington. He would later have a temporary appointment at the Yale University Law School, and building on these and previous legal connections, he was able to be present and active in the formulation of the Genocide Convention at the newly formed United Nations, centered in its early years at Lake Success, New York, and then in Manhattan when the UN's permanent center was moved there.

I refer below to specific provisions of the UN Convention that make it the remarkable document it is, but I turn first to details of Lemkin's personal life as these underscore the fate of the "unsung hero" I've mentioned. When Lemkin died of a heart attack in New York City in 1959—at age fifty-nine; he was born at the turn of the century—he was living alone in a rented room in Manhattan, paid for largely by contributions (gifts, "loans") from friends and acquaintances. His graveside funeral in a cemetery in Queens was attended by seven people; the funeral itself was paid for by the American Jewish Committee. This stark setting marked the end of a man who after early and unusual success as a lawyer in prewar and increasingly antisemitic Poland then—during the war and after it—met with heads of government in Europe and at the United Nations; who had addressed delegate after delegate of UN member countries in order to win agreement for the document on the "prevention and punishment of the crime of genocide" and succeeded not only in that on a vote in the General Assembly, but also subsequently in convincing the national legislatures of twenty countries to ratify individually their respective countries' agreement in the General Assembly. The latter was a condition in the Convention itself (the UN had at the time fifty-seven members), required to be met in a two-year period. By the end of that period the number of ratifications exceeded the number required, a notable achievement since ratification by the twenty individual legislatures was a more difficult matter than the General Assembly vote, involving public discussion in the individual national settings. (The potential obstacles here were epitomized in the United States, which at President Truman's direction had voted for the Convention in the General Assembly in 1948, but failed to ratify the Convention until 1988 and only after the Senate had previously voted *against* ratification; moreover, the Senate's ratification came when it did with a "Reservation" attached stipulating that the United States could be prosecuted under the Convention only with the US consent on the specific occasion—in effect, crippling the Convention's force.) In the course of these efforts, Lemkin was himself nominated for the Nobel Peace Prize—seven times in the 1950s. These accomplishments and their recognition at the time only underscore his straitened circumstances at the time of his death and his relative neglect subsequently.

To be sure, Lemkin's life marks the biography of a single person which, viewed historically—like the other individual histories mentioned before—remains a small part of the cataclysm of World War II and the Holocaust. What he left behind, however—the Convention on Genocide—warrants present and lasting recognition. For Lemkin, the *need* for that legislation was overwhelming, an urgency based in his thinking on four grounds, any one of which would in his view have been sufficient. First was the fact that international law had virtually nothing to say about actions taken by a national government *within* its own boundaries. This meant in effect that any government could legitimately treat minority groups under its rule however it chose to, on the grounds that all such decisions were entirely "internal" matters, thus within the rights of the government, whatever its goals or principles. Minority groups within a country thus had no protection or rights in international law, and this was for Lemkin a serious deficiency.

The second factor discernible in his thinking was that the so-called "fog of war" argument—the cover that wartime typically provided for nations at war—had been used (and in World War II *was* used) to justify the persecution of groups of people both within the warring countries and in territories they conquered. The Geneva Conventions provided some protection for prisoners of war and for the treatment of civilian noncombatants in wartime, but these did not apply in peacetime, and the "fog of war" often was used to justify abuse of the Geneva Conventions' stipulations during wartime itself, especially as members of noncombatant groups became victims, whether intentionally or as the "collateral" damage of unintended consequences.

The third consideration for Lemkin was that in any government, a structure of authority held that allowed anyone below the ruler(s) to justify all actions that they took, whatever their character, on the grounds that they, as subordinates, were only "following orders." This rationalization could be applied to any command actions, and could be (and was) then used as justification for acts which violated the rules of "normal" warfare; it, too, in Lemkin's view, had to be challenged. The fourth of Lemkin's concerns, which in effect underlay *all* the others, was the fundamental value he attached to group-identity and life—the importance of group membership for civilization and culture, and indeed for the *lives* of those within the groups and thus for the existence of the groups themselves. So important was the role of such associations for Lemkin that the destruction of groups became for him a distinctive type and level of murder, one that differed, although it was no less destructive, from the murder of individuals as individuals, criminal as that was and as it had been generally recognized.

In this view of group-identity, Lemkin was going beyond the traditional conception of natural and then more recently human rights, which had virtually without exception emphasized *individual* rights (as in the "unalienable" rights cited in the US Declaration of Independence). By contrast, "genocide" implied recognition that the principle of *group*-rights, the rights of groups to exist, was as basic in political and moral analysis as that of individual rights. (I speak of this as "implied" because the Genocide Convention does not use the phrase "group-rights." But as I discuss further in chapter 8, the latter term and concept have gained increasing currency since 1948, with much of that currency—I argue—due to the Convention on Genocide in its assertion of the murder of groups as a distinctive violation.)

All these considerations, then, Lemkin attempted to take into account in the UN Convention on Genocide, and certain key features of that legislation warrant consideration both for the way they elaborate the concept of genocide and for the issues in that formulation that have been contested, some of which remain unresolved. So, for example, Article 1 of the Convention boldly asserts that "genocide, whether committed in time of peace or in time of war, is a crime under international law." The phrase "in time of peace or in time of war" would protect group-identity both within national boundaries when that identity is threatened by the ruling government as an "internal" matter *and* within or across national boundaries under the cover of the "fog of war" argument.

Article 2 of the Convention specifies the types and modalities of actions that qualify as genocidal. One requirement asserted here is that for all acts of genocide, there need be the "intent" to commit it as a necessary condition—with this pointing to a crucial difference between the act of genocide and other types of killing. In an individual homicide, the difference between the intent to kill and actually killing someone is decisive, but genocide need not be "successful" in order to qualify as genocide—that is, not *all* the group targeted need in fact be killed in order for the charge of genocide to be upheld. The intent alone to accomplish that end suffices, although obviously there must be evidence to support any such charge, evidence that would ordinarily mean that numbers of the group target had indeed been killed. In this connection, it is important to keep in mind that the Nazi genocide remains a paradigm despite the fact that the Nazis *failed* in their intention to make the Jews "disappear from the earth"—paradigmatic in a way that a charge of individual murder could not be if the person attacked were not killed, but wounded and survived or even escaped unscathed.

Article 2 of the Convention also identifies specific groups deemed *eligible* for genocide: that is, "national, ethnical, racial or religious" groups. As discussed previously, this part of the Convention has often been criticized for its exclusion of other significant groups (e.g., political, economic) and because even the groups named might be contested (e.g., as the lines of "racial" identities have been shown to be blurred or even, as some biologists claim, otiose). The point here, however, is that the group-identities cited—whether from within by the groups' own members or externally by others—have also been commonly distinguished for their unusual importance in group and civil life, and that the groups named have often become victims of genocide just because of their identification with one or more of the characteristics named. That other groups might be added or that some of the four might be challenged does not argue against the fact of their common social impact in the past. It seems indisputable that the *perception* of group-identity as based on one or more of these markers has been a significant feature of group-identity historically and thus also of individual members of those groups.

A further stipulation of Article 2 is that genocide can be committed in a variety of ways, with literal (physical) murder only the most obvious among them. Other ways indicated in the Convention include "imposing measures intended to prevent births within the group" and "forcibly transferring children of the group to another group." The latter two conditions underscore the Convention's design to protect the existence of groups: group sterilization, for example, a less extreme measure than actual murder, would ensure the "disappearance" of the group after one generation; nobody would have been actually murdered except the group itself, and that after a generation. Thus, again, the *group* is the primary victim that genocide claims as its object.

Finally, Article 4 of the Convention insists that "Persons committing genocide . . . shall be punished whether they are constitutionally responsible rulers, public officials or private individuals." This stipulation is important in that it rejects unequivocally the defense often given not only in genocide trials but in many others where a recognizable chain of command has figured in the background. Here the defense that "I was only following orders" becomes irrelevant; those who follow orders in committing genocide are also accountable for the act—a broad extension of legal and moral responsibility proportionate to the severity of the crime committed.

We see from the text of the Genocide Convention how brief the Convention itself is: nineteen Articles that are individually also brief. Little is said in them, furthermore, about the "prevention and punishment" of genocide asserted in the Convention's title except for the stipulation that an international judicial structure should be established which would hear and try charges of genocide. This absence might seem a shortcoming of the Convention, but it is one that can surely be made good, and the International Criminal Court, charged with the prosecution of genocide (among other crimes), is a direct consequence of the Genocide Convention and an effort to enforce it. But the crucial importance of the legislation is in the points I have stressed which individually and together represent a path-breaking effort to define a crime that previously had neither a name nor a distinctive identity. Thus the work and accomplishment—and the bequest—of the single figure of Raphael Lemkin.

I have hoped to make clear acknowledgement that certain points of criticism directed at the Convention on Genocide need to be addressed and more importantly, that they *can be* without undermining the main thrust and impact of the Convention. It has often been objected, as has been mentioned here previously, that the Genocide Convention, despite its formal title, has not succeeded in preventing or in punishing occurrences of genocide. It has also been asserted that genocide itself could be defined as a crime by other, more inclusive and precise and thus arguably more useful, concepts—such as "crimes against humanity" or "crimes against peace" (this objection has been considered in chapters 3 and 4) or, as already mentioned, that the four groups specified in the Genocide

Convention as "eligible" for genocide ("national, ethnical, racial or religious") are unduly restrictive or vague. Such objections ought to be addressed and versions of remedies have been proposed here. In the end, however, I would argue still *in defense of "genocide."* That the Convention has not prevented subsequent genocides is arguably a fault (so far as it is one) of *all* legal or moral prohibitions, from the Ten Commandments to laws setting highway speed limits. Those laws and the punishments for their violation may have *some* deterrent value, but even the most severe punishments have not deterred all (for some crimes, it has been argued, *any*) violations; yet the laws remain on the books. One reason for this is that apart from any purpose of deterrence (also from the mooted function of revenge), laws define and affirm common social values. Neither the symbolic nor the moral consequences of laws in the latter role are quantifiable, but the function itself is recognizable and recognized. The fact that no serious efforts have been made in its almost seventy-year history to amend the Genocide Convention may not prove its adequacy but at least attests to its basic relevance. Certain potential alterations or additions have been mentioned here, and others might be added—from the idea of distinguishing *degrees* of genocide to the need for means of enforcing punishments for genocide as well as means of intervening in ongoing genocides or when early warnings of genocide occur. But overriding such additions or changes is the fact that any proposed replacement for "genocide" as an idea and for the event itself as a distinctive crime bears a heavy burden: the need to mark specifically the phenomenon of group-murder that stands at the foundation of the Genocide Convention, Lemkin's monument.

Chapter 7

From Genocide to Group-Rights

Genocide as group-murder, in the meaning of that charge I have been defending here, is most cogently understood as the violation of a right—from an implication that the right violated is predicated of, *belongs to*, the group victimized. This step asserted in the cause of "group-rights" seems unavoidable on political or social theories that accept the notion of rights of any sort, whether they are claimed to be natural or conventional in their origins; it also, as key to the assertion of group-rights, entails notable expansion in the concept of natural rights that had traditionally been ascribed only to individuals, not groups. Analysis of the connection between genocide and group-rights must then also address the troubled and troubling status of rights as such, even if my focus here is limited within that broad category. The strong position on group-rights—one I defend here—is that the claim that groups have rights to "x," "y," or "z" has grounds identical or analogous to those at the basis of rights ascribed to individuals (although not necessarily to the same ones or in the same order). And the object of genocide makes clear what the "x" involved in it is: because its charge designates the murder of a group, that violation implies a right to existence

137

for "the group" whose destruction had been effected, whatever criteria are used for defining the eligible group.

This implication of a group-right as underlying the concept of genocide has been largely ignored in analyses of that concept; Raphael Lemkin himself only hinted at the broader connection. The reasons for this general neglect warrant further discussion, but whatever could be concluded from it would not blur the fact that Lemkin's conceptualization of "genocide" was and remains a key factor—and Lemkin himself a founder—in the largely post–World War II and post-Lemkin, and ongoing, development of the concept and practice of group-rights. The history of that evolution, even in its relatively short span, is too complex to consider here, but something should be said about the even larger topic of rights talk more generally. Here my discussion moves in two directions: first, in recognizing the origin of "natural" rights theory as that was articulated by the seventeenth and eighteenth century Enlightenment thinkers who propelled the theory into its later applications in political liberalism; and second, noting the evolution of natural rights theory from its initial emphasis on individual rights *as natural* to modified conceptions of the alternate views of the status of rights as conventional or positive, and then currently, most often, as "*human* rights," a phrase which attempts to avoid commitment to either side of the traditionally sharply divided alternatives. The expansion here has gone from exclusive reference in rights talk to individuals who "have" rights to attributing them (including quite different ones) also to groups. (Is the post–World War II shift from "natural" to "human" rights more than a nominal difference? Whatever other reasons pertain, the shift reflects unease with the concept of the "natural," as it then fudges the question of whether the rights referred to are innate or constructed as conventions.) Many rights reasserted under the newer title might be argued for on either of those grounds, but as those grounds also make various claims (some of them incompatible with others), so do the justifications they provide.

An essential feature of natural rights for the seventeenth and eighteenth century thinkers who strongly influenced the subsequent development of the concept—Hugo Grotius, Thomas Hobbes, John Locke—was the emphasis they placed on the status of such rights as individual, *belonging* to the individual innately, naturally, inalienably. These were so tightly bound to the individual person as to make the epithet "possessive individualism" later applied to this view a literal description. Rights defined in this way could of course be violated (thus, too, the individual whose rights they were), but this contingency did not alter the fact of the right itself. So, in the rights to "life, liberty, and the pursuit of happiness" asserted in the United States' Declaration of Independence (1776), the emphasis on the rights of their *individual* holders becomes most explicit in the last of those named—the "pursuit of happiness" as records show that that phrase was substituted by drafters of the document for the earlier claim of a right to "property," with the character of *individual* possession there still more prominent. This same emphasis on the individual "man" as then reiterated in the French Declaration of the Universal Rights of Man and Citizen (1789) was linked both systematically and historically with the social contract theory of the origins of the state and civil government. On that theory, signatories of the contract freely (i.e., individually) after the "original" contract at least tacitly agree to certain limitations on their individual natural rights in return for the security and other benefits afforded by the state—benefits also to be enjoyed, however, individually. Even the limits of government power, once that was agreed to, were understood to be judged individually. If the founding "contract" were violated by a ruler, the individual signatory of the contract, singly or by joining others, had the right to displace and replace the rulers, even by means of revolution. Thus, again, from the origins of the state, through the enjoyment of its benefits, and even in the face of tests posed by its corruption, the *individual* citizen would be at the center of the network, standing on his natural rights.

The modern emergence of the concept of group-rights as adhering to certain groups in the same way that rights belong to individual persons began on an international scale in the context and aftermath of World War I, in response to the issue of the status of displaced minority populations and of minority populations even in accepting host countries that had nonetheless begun to find their own voices. It was in that setting that Woodrow Wilson included among his Fourteen Points proclamation the principle of national self-determination which, as an echo of the principle of *individual* autonomy, ascribed that right—here elevated to national autonomy—also to national groups. This proposal understandably triggered difficult discussions at the time and subsequently about the conditions that would-be national groups would have to meet in order to be eligible for self-determination— first, in the question of criteria by which groups would qualify (the numbers of people seeking it? a defined geographical space? ethnic distinctiveness?). The second consideration would be the question about which other rights might accrue to minority groups with—or arguably more importantly, even in the absence of—national self-determination. The latter issue becomes especially pressing for minorities that remain within a larger (majority) culture, encountering questions on matters like linguistic, educational, and cultural rights that although at times associated with the assertion of political national self-determination do not necessarily presuppose that.

Also the conceptual and systemic issues related to group-rights as such are severe. Conflicts may occur among such rights both within an individual group and between the rights of one group and those of others— together with conflicts between group and individual rights in both those contexts. (So, for example, the potential difference between an individual's "right of exit" as it may at times conflict with a *group's* "right to exist," as the latter could be threatened by a diminishing populace.) That there may be no comprehensive solution to such conflicts on the basis of the definition of group-rights is, however, no more an objection to the general claim for group-rights than the common conflicts among individual rights are (as, for example, between the right to free expression and the right to security). Thus again, there is a direct parallel between the affirmations of individual and group-rights; Jeremy Bentham's caustic reference to claims of individual rights as "nonsense upon stilts" would surely have been applied to group-rights as well if the concept of such rights had come before him. And if solutions that have been proposed for the problems that Bentham found in the concept of rights are unlikely to have persuaded him, the question also remains of the extent to which the utilitarian alternative proposed by Bentham and his successors *overcomes its* problems. Classic ethical and political theories as in Plato and Aristotle also find their way with no reference to rights, individual or collective, and with an arguably still more significant criticism of rights theories. But the scrutiny of alternatives to rights theories in general extends farther than the discussion here can go.

That rights ("natural" or "human" or even as "constructed") have been variously identified individually may not itself suffice as justification for continuing to think within the framework of rights theories, but it shows sufficient flexibility within that framework to allow rights advocates, including those of group-rights, to respond to many of the problems critics have found there. Here as elsewhere, and not only in basic philosophical positions, it is evident that there are no free lunches: the strong positive basis for group-rights, evident in the grounds for defining the crime of genocide, emerges as at least as weighty as criticism of it and the alternatives that such criticism proposes. The claim of rights as a type of philosophical sublimation or "as if"—an epiphenomenon—has an obvious attraction, especially as bearing on group-rights (as discussed in relation to Larry May's position on group-rights in chapter 3); but again, and perhaps finally, an argument from analogy holds here, at least minimally—the group-right implied in the crime of genocide is directly parallel to the crime asserted in individual murder: a right to life or existence for the group as group beside the right to life or existence for individuals as individuals.

As already noted, Lemkin himself, when he initially claimed the identification of genocide as a crime, did not elaborate on its basis as the violation of a *right*. But the connection was not far off, and subsequently he spoke of it in those terms explicitly. Lemkin not only emphasized the character of genocide as at times a "double murder," but went beyond that. So, for example, in a letter to Trygve Lie, then Secretary General of the United Nations (May 20, 1946), he wrote about his campaign on behalf of the concept of genocide: "By formulating genocide as a crime, the principle has been proclaimed that a national, racial or religious group as an entity has *the right* to exist, analogously as the recognition of homicide as a crime proclaims the principles that an individual has a right to live" (emphasis added, Lemkin Papers, Box 1/13 American Jewish Archives). Even here, however, he did not specifically address the nascent concept of group-rights in general that he was in fact proposing for one such particular right.

Lemkin's work on the issue of group-murder culminated in the Convention on the Punishment and Prevention of the Crime of Genocide that specified the several types of "genos" or group deserving protection against the crime of (group) murder. When previous advocacy of minority rights had been initiated, it had been almost entirely addressed to minorities within countries, not across international boundaries. And for Lemkin, it was the absence of international protection for threatened groups, *whether within or across* national boundaries, that required a remedy. Thus the wording of the Genocide Convention as it was adopted, "to prevent and punish" acts of destruction aimed at "national, ethnical, racial or religious" groups, wherever and whenever they were threatened with annihilation. Again, with reference to threats in which the existence of a *group* was threatened, with the clear implication that the group attacked had a right to exist apart from any rights their members had as individuals. The concept of rights is thus expanded among those who "have" them from individuals to groups.

That this violation of a group-right found force in the definition of genocide as distinct from the violation of individual rights follows from two specific items of evidence. The first is the distinction implied by genocide between that act and mass murder. That distinction, as has been argued previously, is not a matter of the relative number of victims (there may be as many or more victims in the latter); genocide depends on the essential feature of the victims' identity in relation to a group—in contrast to the atrocity of mass murder in which, although the victims can certainly be numbered and even characterized by the physical setting, the factor of a group-identity is either entirely absent or only incidental. The second item of evidence is the stipulation in the definition provided by the Genocide Convention that genocide would apply to the annihilation of a group also by means other than physical murder, as for example, by "forcibly preventing births within a group" or by the "deportation of children" (Article 4). Both the latter means would ensure the disappearance of the group (after a generation), but without physical murder, and the wrong committed here, then, would be against the group's right to exist in the future—established in the present about the future, to be sure, but still pointing to its annihilation.

It is difficult to imagine that the conceptualization of genocide could have had the impact that it has had if the term and concept added nothing to accounts of even the atrocity of mass murder that had a long, well-documented history *as* massacre or mass murder. Certainly the Genocide Convention has been the object of criticism, and indeed even a number of the nations that ratified the Convention attached qualifying reservations, some of them severe, that limit their commitment to the scope of the Convention. But it is also clear that the principal force of the Convention in its identification of a distinctive crime has been a significant counterweight to all such proposed alterations and certainly to the prospect of its outright repeal or nullification.

It is undeniable that acts of genocide have occurred since the United Nations adopted the Genocide Convention as well as before it—in Cambodia, Rwanda, Bosnia. And some critics regard those crimes as evidence of flaws in the Convention itself. (So, for example, the political commentator Edward Luttwak, after first disputing the characterization of the Armenian massacres by the Turks as genocide, turns against the Genocide Convention itself: "I spit on it, given all the difference it has made to the fate of the Cambodians, Rwandan Tutsis, Sarajevo Bosnians.") Without addressing the question of how the deterrent effect of *any* legislation can be determined (still more difficult in this instance because of the UN's weak powers of enforcement), the same criticism would hold other laws failures (thus, also to be erased?) for the many acts of individual murder, rape, or robbery that occur in jurisdictions with laws against them, jurisdictions that in contrast to that of the UN *have* established and ready means of enforcement.

A recent development related to the role of the Genocide Convention and a significant step in the direction of its enforcement was the activation in 2002 of the

International Criminal Court, a standing judicial body whose formal charge includes first among others the prosecution of crimes of genocide. (There are three other charges to the Court for prosecution: crimes against humanity, war crimes, and the crime of aggression.) Here, now, is an international court, as prescribed in the Genocide Convention, empowered by 123 signatory nations (as of February 2015—among whom the United States remains notably absent) to judge and punish violations of what can only be understood as a group-right to its existence, within or across national boundaries and irrespective of whether the violations are committed by nations, other groups, or individuals. It is a matter of record that other significant UN resolutions that addressed the issue of human rights simultaneously with or after the Genocide Convention (e.g., the Universal Declaration of Human Rights [1948] and the Covenant on Civil and Political Rights [1966]) have avoided the terminology of group-rights, with the single exception of the right of national self-determination. An immediate reason for this omission was undoubtedly the difficulty, conceptual and practical, of specifying the criteria that would define the eligible groups—a difficulty already encountered in relation to the groups named in the Genocide Convention. A secondary and derivative problem, one that has become more prominent as the right of self-determination has been acted on or threatened since World War II, is that of defining the means for sustaining group-identities, whether through self-determination or, for minority groups that do not achieve full self-determination, by some form of cultural (and linguistic) freedom, educational systems, as well (on a different front) by admitting claims for reparations in light of prior violations. (One instance of reparation in this sense has appeared—and been contested—in the United States under the loose rubric of Affirmative Action.)

The requirements and even the strengths of group-rights theory bring with them costs that engender varied and at time severe problems, both practical and conceptual. The most basic of these appears in the questions of which groups are to have such rights and how that determination is to be made; then too, there is the question of the extent of such rights—an issue that is heightened as the rights of one group may conflict with those of another and as conflicts may occur *between* individual and group-rights. If the conceptualization of genocide has added its force to the concept of group-rights, then these problems too have been imposed in that same bequest, providing grist for critics who would reject outright or severely limit the claims of group-rights as such. But here, it seems, two rejoinders support those claims and, in my view, still more strongly. First, justifications for *individual* rights face many, if not all the same problems that justifications for group-rights do, including the questions of where they originate, who decides on them, the range of their application, and to whom they belong. Second, the political and moral choices faced—humanly, nationally, internationally—are not between problem-ridden theories of rights, on the one hand, and on the other hand, a problem-free political discourse capable of resolving the hard questions of international justice *without* reference to rights. What Lemkin set in motion through the concept of genocide was a procedure for addressing urgent and recurrent political and social issues in the particular setting of groups in a way intended to preserve a basic means of *both* cultural and individual expression, cultural and individual self-realization. All we need do to understand the emphasis placed by this on the value of group-identity in human lives is to attempt to imagine those lives (*ours*) in the absence of such groups.

These, then, are some of the problems that the practice and implementation of group-rights raise in comparison to the problems of thinking politically and morally without them. If there had been any doubts about this before the twentieth century, that century's history dispelled them by brute force. Even that force, however, required Lemkin's moral imagination and indefatigable efforts to describe for the world what had happened before its eyes. Everyone would undoubtedly prefer a world in which there was no need for laws like the Genocide Convention or institutions like the International Criminal Court. But that happens not to have been the world Lemkin lived in—nor is it the world we now inhabit.

Arendt on the Evil in Genocide

Banality's Depths

Anything one says now about Hannah Arendt extensive writings will probably have been said previously, and with all that has been written specifically about her *Eichmann in Jerusalem: A Report on the Banality of Evil*, now more than fifty years old, repetition (including some of one's own work) becomes almost inevitable; even *mis*interpretation and disagreement are finally variants of repetition. But as Kierkegaard in his hopeful view of *Repetition* finds "repetition forward" a possibility and contrast to the usual "repetition *backward*," I aim for something like that here.

Thus into the "depths" of banality. The US presidential election in 1964, contested between the then sitting President, Lyndon Johnson and his Republican challenger, Barry Goldwater, is remembered now mainly for a series of gaffes by Goldwater that contributed to his overwhelming defeat (he won only six of the fifty states). After one such gaffe, an incredulous reporter asked a member of Goldwater's entourage what Goldwater was *really* like, deep down. The response was memorable: "Well, deep down he's shallow." Whether or not that applied to Goldwater, I propose its opposite here, claiming that the concept of banality as Arendt inscribes it in the subtitle of her book, *Eichmann in Jerusalem*, and then applies and amplifies it in the book itself, is not itself shallow or "banal" but deep (to some extent in Arendt's own terms, but also in ways she does not address and would possibly not find congenial). Indeed, it is in ways sufficiently deep to reveal a number of also deep problems in the view she defends there of evil's banality itself.

I consider Arendt's book here only in what became its final form so far as she controlled it—that is, in its second edition (1965) which supplemented the first (book) edition of May 1963 by the addition of a "Postscript" in which she reflected on some of the criticism directed at her original *New Yorker* pieces and the first edition. Arendt herself claimed that aside from the Postscript itself and her account in the text of the assassination attempt on Hitler of July 20, 1944, the second edition included only "technical" changes to the first, although the erasure in 1965 of her earlier reference to Rabbi Leo Baeck of Berlin as the "Jewish Fuhrer" indicates that at least *that* change was more than "technical." Nonetheless, the second edition is the book as she left it and as we have it—and except for one reference, I focus on that text alone, without relating it to other of her writings, prior or subsequent. I understand that this restriction entails a more general theory of reading and literary interpretation which I don't attempt to elaborate here. *Eichmann in Jerusalem* was published by Arendt as a "text-in-itself"—and although in it she mentions other authors' accounts of Nazi history and of issues related to the Eichmann trial, she makes no reference to her own earlier work nor does she cite any of it in the extensive bibliography she attaches to the book. And of course she could not have cited her own *future* writings. At least initially, then, it seems warranted to read the text as she wrote and stood by it, and as it remains now, whatever qualifications might otherwise be attached by way of backshadowing or foreshadowing from her earlier or later works.

The one exception to this interpretive restriction appears in a brief paragraph that I cite, written by Arendt soon after the publication of the first edition. This statement comes in a letter from Arendt to Gershom Scholem, dated July 24, 1963, on the cusp of what became the break between them (itself unbroken after that), and at a point of entry into what I am calling the "depths" of banality. After disputing a number of specific faults that Scholem had alleged in the Eichmann book (and, ad hominem, in her), Arendt responds quite differently to his objection to the distinction she had emphasized between "radical" evil and evil as "banal":

> [About this] you are quite right: I changed my mind and do no longer speak of "radical evil." . . . It is indeed my opinion now that evil is never "radical," that it is only extreme, and that it possesses neither depth nor any demonic dimension. It can overgrow and lay waste the whole world precisely because it spreads like a fungus on the surface. It is 'thought-defying,' as I said because thought tries to reach some depth, to go to the roots, and the moment it concerns itself with evil, it is frustrated because there is nothing. That is its 'banality.' Only the good has depth and can be radical.

No similarly explicit, concise yet sweeping, statement about evil—*or* good—appears in *Eichmann in Jerusalem*

itself, and although it might be argued that the book's subject was Eichmann and his trial rather than moral or ethical theory as such (Arendt herself asserts in the book that
"finally and least of all [is the book] a theoretical treatise
on the nature of evil"), she does move widely in the book
to detail the means as well as the effects of the Nazi genocide across Europe and of the actions of a number of individual perpetrators (many of them less heavily implicated
in Nazi criminality than Eichmann) to such an extent that
a general theory might be inferred. But questions about
the nature of moral freedom and the choices implied by it,
although hinted at, are not confronted directly even in her
several references to the 1945 Nuremberg trials, including the first one which involved the highest-ranking Nazi
officials captured by the Allies. Quite pointedly, when
she *does* contrast Eichmann with the many undisputed
demonic agents of evildoing available, she cites none of
the many *historical* villains whom she could have cited,
but Shakespeare's *fictional* models: Iago, Macbeth, and
most consistently, Richard III, who in Shakespeare's antic-
ipation of what would later surface in Kant as Radical Evil,
intended to "prove [himself] a villain." Limiting as this
choice of examples is, it underscores Arendt's continuing effort to counter the inclination among many viewers
of the trial (perhaps also as a reminder to herself) who
would number Eichmann among the demonic or satanic
group of great moral villains—an association which in her
view was no less misplaced than it was common. Was this
choice of fictional rather than historical evildoers to exemplify Radical Evil significant? Almost certainly, although
she does not herself comment on this. Nor does she, after
altering her view on Radical Evil in the statement she

wrote to Scholem concede that with this revision also Iago and Richard III would then exemplify banal rather than radical evil. (If this omission is meant to imply that radical evil as she had earlier found it exemplified could *only* be fictional, this seems an oddly offhanded way of making an important substantive point.)

Admittedly, angular glimpses of ethical theory hover over Arendt's account of the Eichmann trial. Once viewers of the trial or readers of her book get past the dramatic image of the "man in the glass booth," the fact of his ordinariness becomes not only unmistakable but casts a broader shadow than that of a single figure in the event. The efforts of the prosecution, principally of Gideon Hausner whom Arendt criticizes sharply, to identify Eichmann the individual with the totality of Nazi atrocities had constantly to contend with the man himself and his formulaic, *banal* responses to the charges and questions posed by the prosecution and the three-judge court. And quite apart from that, the very *idea* of entering into a formal discussion with a single person charged with responsibility in the death of millions of Jews in the setting of a court established by a Jewish state and making a sustained effort to follow juridical rules of procedural fairness itself ensured a notable disproportion between the effect and the alleged cause.

The concept of banality, then, seems ready-made for Eichmann in the term's conventional meaning of ordinary, commonplace, pedestrian. But Arendt, impatient with this obvious connotation, quickly insists that her own use of the term is deeper than that even if not exclusive of it. So she repeatedly calls attention to Eichmann's reliance on clichés—those linguistic tics with the status of currency, addictive like all habits because they are effortless, requiring no thought and thus "thoughtless." Few speakers or writers entirely escape their lure, but there are obvious differences in degrees of dependence on them, and Arendt finds them so prominent a part of Eichmann's expressing himself that this dependence seems even comic to her: "It was difficult indeed," she writes, "not to suspect that he was a clown."

The most striking instance of what Arendt means by this comes near the end of both her book and Eichmann's life. In that connection, she notes that Eichmann "went to the gallows with great dignity" and then cites his last words as reported, presumably addressed most immediately to the witnesses (she was not herself present): "After a short while, gentlemen, we shall all meet again. Such is the fate of all men. Long live Germany! Long live Argentina! Long live Austria! I shall not forget them." That last sentence was uttered by a man moments away from forgetting not only them but *everything* and presumably aware of this. Any anthology of "last words" might reserve a special place for these—which also typify what Arendt refers to in her own coinage as Eichmann's "clowneries."

This reliance by Eichmann on clichés—in phrase and thought—turns out, however, to be more symptom than substance for Arendt as she moves on to the deeper meaning of banality. What such dependence represents and expresses in its more significant way is the "thoughtlessness" impelling it, which becomes for her a key term in understanding Eichmann and the quality of banality. Recall that she describes her ascription of banality in Eichmann as evident "strictly at the factual level, pointing to a phenomenon that stared one in the face at the trial. . . . He

[Eichmann] merely, to put the matter colloquially, never realized what he was doing, thus the interdependence of thoughtlessness and evil." In this assessment she emphasizes the difference between thoughtlessness and stupidity, which might otherwise be confused. The latter she explicitly rules out as characterizing Eichmann: "He was not stupid. It was sheer thoughtlessness—something by no means identical with stupidity—that predisposed him to become one of the greatest criminals of that period."

In a recent attack on Arendt's judgment of Eichmann at the trial and beyond, the German scholar Bettina Stangneth—enlarging on a criticism of Arendt's "banality" which originated almost immediately with her book's publication—has claimed that the Eichmann in Jerusalem on whom Arendt bases her account was in effect an imposter, acting a role for the occasion and in direct conflict with his strong commitment to Nazi ideology and antisemitism, as evidenced in his history in the SS before and during the war and then also afterward in his Argentinian refuge. Stangneth thus contends that Eichmann was consciously and unapologetically a deeply (one also assumes "thoughtfully") committed Nazi. Arendt did not have access to much of the material on which Stangneth bases her analysis, but even so, Stangneth's deconstruction of Eichmann in the Glass Box is not the only or arguably the most plausible conclusion to be drawn from the additional material she cites. Putting aside the question of how Eichmann managed to play the role enacted on Stangneth's account—deceiving his Israeli interrogators and the psychiatrists who had access to him prior to the trial and the judges at the trial itself—Stangneth does not consider even as a possibility that Eichmann's role playing—if such it was—might well have begun long before that, in his Nazi history as well (there certainly are specific matters on which Stangneth takes Eichmann at his [then] word which turn out to be false—for one example, his professed knowledge of Hebrew and Yiddish). Furthermore, even if we accept Stangneth's claim about Eichmann's lying about his antisemitism when he was on trial (it is after all a standard trope of many antisemites to deny any *personal* animus), his interrogation there and previously points to an explanation compatible with both her claim and Arendt's banality thesis: that while he had an active role in the destruction of the European Jews, he was at the same time and no less deeply concerned with the advancement of his own career and the lack of recognition that had been and was accorded him. One needn't argue about the evident disproportion between these two motives or even of how much greater one was for him since the two could have readily worked side by side. As they well might have in the years before Germany's defeat and even in Eichmann's years in Argentina as his Nazi credentials and beliefs warmed a place for him there in his circle. And as it could have also in the Jerusalem courtroom. In none of those contexts, does role-playing or its "natural" duplicity preclude thoughtlessness or banality in Arendt's specific use of those terms. That Eichmann expressed a commitment to Nazi ideology and acted on it is no more proof of his reflective powers than it would be for many other "thoughtless" ideologues.

In common usage, "thoughtlessness"—like banality—refers to individual acts, often small offenses that might easily have been avoided by the agent who committed them (for example, as someone might "comfort" a mourner by speaking of death as a "release"). Again, this is *not* what

Arendt primarily means by the term, although what she does mean becomes increasingly opaque in the course of her book as she continues to avoid her own alternative to it and *its* implications. Eichmann, she writes, did not *think* about what he was doing, with that failure leading him to speak and more than that, act as he did: "thought-defying." And the single most important implication of that view of Eichmann is a counterfactual that Arendt herself does not mention: namely, that if he had not been "thoughtless"— that is, if he had thought about his actions and their consequences—he would not have done or said what he did. If "not thinking" was responsible for his speech and actions, then reversing that source—*thinking*—would or at least could have taken him in a different direction. "Thoughtfulness" is thus at least a sufficient and perhaps a necessary condition for not only avoiding evil's banality but even avoiding evildoing as such.

This is a sweeping claim, and Arendt never asserts it explicitly—but it emerges as a clear implication of her view of evil's banality and of that concept's depth. Philosophically, it should be noted, this view has important historical precedents, specifically in the rationalist tradition, classically exemplified in Plato's dialogues (as in Books VI and VII of the *Republic* and in the *Gorgias*), with Plato's stand-in, Socrates, arguing that to know the good is *to do* the good: knowledge as a both sufficient and necessary condition for avoiding evildoing. A person who really *knows*, who reasons the way to the Good in a given setting will act accordingly. Conversely, to do wrong or evil is to act from ignorance, not by *choosing* evil, but because the agent does not know any better. On this view and much in Arendt's terms in her letter to Scholem, thinking, when it attempts to address or analyze evil, finds "nothing" there—with "nothing" a synonym for the Platonic view of evil as privation, emptiness, nonexistence. If "mud" has no place in the world of forms, as Plato says in the *Parmenides*, evil certainly would not. Mud and fungus, after all, have much in common, certainly more than mud or fungus do with the form of the Good.

The modern rationalist position, in figures like Spinoza and Leibniz, provides more recent iterations of this view, and have similarly been challenged by some of the earlier objections, the most benign of them arguing that what it asserts is finally no more than a tautology: on its claim that true knowledge requires the subordination of all other impulses of the self to reason, then of course, actions related to that knowledge follow necessarily, with no space between the two. Thus the claim is true by hypothesis. And then, too, in opposition hardly less strong appears the professedly empirical objection in the counterclaim of Paul: "That which I know I ought not to do, I do, and that which I know I ought to do, I do not" (Romans, 7:15). However compelling knowledge of the good is, in Paul's words, it at times proves insufficient for withstanding an opposing but no less real internal source.

Whether or how Arendt's conception of evil's banality as related to individual wrongdoing fits between these extremes remains finally unsettled (and unsettling) in report of *Eichmann in Jerusalem*. As Eichmann on trial is central to that account, furthermore, the question of the relationship between individual responsibility and evil in its banality becomes itself part of this crux. In what sense can "thoughtlessness" in the causal role Arendt assigns it be considered a choice? And if it is not a choice, with the implication which then follows that thoughtlessness is involuntary, any claim ascribing personal or individual responsibility becomes problematic. Kant did not flinch at the parallel question in locating the origins of Radical Evil in his extreme version of that phenomenon; its source for him involved individual agency and will, no less than adherence to the Categorical Imperative did in the opposite direction. But just as a question persists of how compelling that Kantian resolution is, so also the question persists of how, on Arendt's account, thoughtlessness—if involuntary—be a moral ground and cause of even "banal" evildoing.

I conclude these comments on certain ways and means of evil with two general comments and one that revisits the depths of banality. The first comment concerns the absence in Arendt's book of the role of the imagination in thinking or, for Eichmann, in his thoughtlessness. Arendt does refer once to the failure of Eichmann's "moral imagination," describing this as his inability to "put himself in the place of another." But as the role of the imagination is typically viewed through its aesthetic rather than its moral consequences, the status of the *immoral* imagination, as in conceiving and implementing elements of the so-called "Final Solution," has been largely neglected in *both* its aesthetic and moral aspects. The Nazi genocide required few technical innovations as imagination might otherwise be required for them; that it was so markedly "low-tech"—with its means readily explicable—might, in Arendt's terms, add to the impress of its banality. On the other hand, neglect of the role of the imagination in the Nazi genocide is not exceptional; in both philosophical and theological historical surveys of the "practice" of evil, evil appears as driven by a constant and unvarying thoughtless human impulse. It is as though the "evil inclination" ("Yetzer ha'rah") cited in *Genesis*, or Original Sin in the Christian narrative appear in those accounts as settling the character of human evildoing once and for all, with any apparent variations later viewed only as instantiations of the original.

But there is a compelling argument for a "progressive" theory of the history of evildoing parallel to the common claims of a progression in moral enlightenment; here the artfulness of evildoing would also be creative and accretive. It seems in these terms a failure of imagination to describe the details of the "Final Solution" without recognizing the imaginative strokes fostering them that extend beyond the "solution" only of extermination. Commonplace examples of that source appear even in the so-called punishment cells at Auschwitz: cells so constricted that the prisoner could do nothing but stand, cells in which the prisoner was sentenced to total darkness and silence, others in which the prisoner could hear only the commands and shots of the firing squad in the narrow space of the execution ground immediately outside. These appear, of course, aside from the inventive techniques of overt torture or the numerous other and slighter examples of what Primo Levi termed "useless violence": punishable bed-making requirements (for what were only marginally beds), the requisite number of seven buttons on men's shirts (with no means provided for compliance), and the Jewish band accompaniment (playing German music otherwise forbidden to Jewish musicians) to the daily departure and arrival of labor groups and the slogans on the value of cleanliness posted over the few, often disabled, sinks. None of these instances, from large to small, are *entailed* by the goal of the "Final Solution"; it required (and was given) additional time and effort to imagine them, to go beyond the direct means to a single-minded end. This aspect of the "Final Solution" is a basis for the claim I have proposed elsewhere that perpetrators of the Nazi evil must themselves have been conscious of the evil in their actions even as they were committing them: an unexpected rehearsal of Paul's words.

The second general comment concerns the absence in Arendt's conception of the banality of evil of any reference to the "banality of good." For surely, Arendt's own definition of evil's banality—thoughtlessness, a refusal or inability to think on the part of an agent—also attends actions or conduct that commonly (thoughtlessly) are regarded by both agents and observers as good: acting "morally" in order to ensure earthly or heavenly rewards, the demand for justice as a substitute for revenge, philanthropy practiced for the sake of public recognition. Even in ascribing evildoing to Eichmann, Arendt allowed him the "reasoned" motive of self-advancement, and that seems no less a feature of these varied efforts for a supposed good: less dramatic than the banality of evil, but nonetheless (perhaps because of that pallor) worth noting as a companion to it.

The concluding point to which I call attention stems from Arendt's own concluding words in her book's epilogue. Arendt had expressed herself earlier in the text as critical of procedures in the Eichmann trial on several counts, principally in relation to the court's constitution and the prosecution's formulation of charges against Eichmann. But on the punishment imposed by the judges at the trial and later confirmed by the five-judge appeals court, she fully agreed. Her justification for Eichmann's execution, however, differs from that of the courts, and the way in which her justification relates to the "banality of evil" brings together a number of the issues already raised here. Arendt herself writes the last words of a speech that she would have liked to hear from the two sets of judges as justification for the death sentence imposed on Eichmann: "Just as you [Eichmann] supported and carried out a policy of not wanting to share the earth with the Jewish people and the people of a number of other nations . . . we find that no one, that is, no member of the human race, can be expected to want to share the earth with you. This is the reason, and the only reason, you must hang."

Even allowing for a rhetorical flourish at the conclusion of her "report on the banality of evil," this statement goes beyond any ground or basis in Arendt's previous analysis; namely, that *anyone* not wanting to share the earth with the Jewish people—or, in presumably generalizable, with any *other* people—ought also to share Eichmann's fate. The latter implication would entail the prospect of hanging hundreds of thousands of active German agents and supporters of Hitler; if applied as a principle to agents and supporters of other recent genocides, it would have a much wider reach. And the numerous historical instances of genocide cited by Lemkin would extend that further still, even if only retroactively. Has there been a more graphic design for genocide than the biblical order commanding Israel to destroy not only the people and descendants of Amalek but also their *memory?* (The turns of irony surface here as well, if we recall the

Nazi plans for a Jewish Museum in Prague to depict an "extinct" race: they assembled material for the museum at the same time they were attempting to make extinct the people who created that material and much of the material itself.)

This implication is not itself a counterargument to Arendt's conclusion, although it warrants further scrutiny. And still more fundamentally, in what way is Arendt's justification for Eichmann's hanging linked to, let alone entailed by her thesis of evil's banality? At first glance, her justification for Eichmann's execution seems only an extension of the principle of an "eye for an eye"—*lex talionis*—with all the crudity of that principle. But more, and more significantly, it raises again the question of the nature of individual responsibility for evildoing. One could hardly advocate Arendt's justification for the death sentence on the basis of her claims for Eichmann's "thoughtlessness," his inability to think—unless *that* had in some sense been a choice on his part, his responsibility. Eichmann, in other words, must have *chosen* to be Eichmann and thus to do as Eichmann did. But could a choice of such magnitude and with such crushing consequences have been the outcome only of *thoughtlessness?* Would his thoughtlessness itself then have been a choice? And if not, if all that he did stemmed from an incapacity on Eichmann's part, how would hanging him be justified as a fit measure for that? In this sense, the price of banality as Arendt conceives it turns out to be higher and more demanding, and deeper, than she herself acknowledged.

Chapter 9

Genocide-Denial

The very enormity of genocide nudges us towards incredulity, towards denial and refusal.

Primo Levi, *La Stampa*, January 19, 1979

Everyone is free to interpret a phenomenon like the Hitlerian genocide according to his philosophy. . . . Everyone is free, up to the limit, to imagine or to dream that these monstrous facts did not take place. They unfortunately did take place, and no one can deny their existence without outrage to the truth. . . .

Statement by thirty-four French historians,
Le Monde, February 21, 1979

But of course there *have* been denials and debates, about *all* the recent atrocities alleged to have been genocides: the massacre of Armenians by Turks in 1915–17 no less than the attempt to "disappear" the Jews by the Nazis between 1941 and 1945; the slaughter in Rwanda by the Hutu of their Tutsi "neighbors" as well as some of their own tribesmen in 1994; and the systematic campaign against Cambodian minorities by Pol Pot and the Khmer Rouge in 1975–79. It is not only that the perpetrators themselves in these instances have often denied committing these crimes—or the criminality of whatever acts of theirs they acknowledged—but that others, with less self-serving motives, have at times spoken to the same effect, arguing that although atrocities were committed in those events, they did not meet the criteria of genocide. A sufficient number of these instances of Denial have accrued to bring to light a family resemblance among them, a characteristic pattern—and it is important to identify that pattern for the purposes of both understanding and confronting it.

For all the genocides alleged that have been denied, four principal claims have figured separately or in combination as "evidence" for the case thus made. The first of these asserts that the alleged number of victims in the genocide has been exaggerated—with the implication that a lesser number, typically a *much* lesser number, weakens the claim of the genocide at issue as an organized plan. The lesser number, if conceded, would open the way both to continuing revision of the numbers and to the charge of genocide as such. The second claim holds that the methods cited as causes or means of annihilation are mistaken and/or implausible (in effect fictions). So, for a major example from the Nazi genocide, Denial that the gas chambers that have come forward as a central, iconic means of the genocide *could* have physically or mechanically killed the number of victims alleged. The third argument proposes that such crimes as did occur in the genocide alleged took place in the "fog of war" (whether civil war or international), with the implication that since wartime atrocities occur commonly and unavoidably, the atrocities grouped here together under the heading of genocide should be understood by way of that explanation. In any event—this defense goes on—whatever happens in warfare is the responsibility of the individuals engaged, not the strategic or political leaders, and wartime accountability, under the "fog," becomes impossible to determine. Fourth—most broadly and basically—that whatever atrocities occurred in the event at issue did not represent an overall genocidal intent (accepted as a necessary condition for the crime of genocide); that whatever occurred did so with no covering or overall design. In other words, that the atrocities committed were local, disconnected from others—and even if not *that*, motivated by other, more limited goals than that of group extermination. (I do not include here denials based on rejection of the concept of genocide as such, as discussed in chapters 3 and 4; Denial typically accepts the concept and phenomenon of genocide in general, only denying the claim of a specific occurrence.)

Each of the four claims noted has been asserted and disputed in particular instances, although this by itself does not distinguish such Denials from the way in which conflicts arise and sides are taken in many historical disputes. In this sense, Genocide-Denial, like such other historical disputes, must answer finally to the weight of evidence and interpretation. Whatever else can be said about their motives or circumstances, the charges made by Genocide-Deniers revolve around historical claims without which the charges themselves would be meaningless—an implication granted by the advocates of any specific Denial as well as by their critics. That basis involves positions drawn from empirical evidence, and although the reach of such evidence is invariably limited, assessment of the evidence is assumed at least to extend to those limits. The assessment of Denial claims is in this sense quite straightforward, no different procedurally from the assessment of any other historical or legal position. On the other hand, distinctive questions do arise on the periphery of Genocide-Denial that bear also on its historical assessment, although seldom recognized in relation to it; these warrant consideration on their own and are the focus of the discussion here.

The six questions I consider as marking this periphery are not meant to preclude, let alone to deny, Genocide-Denial itself (extrahistorical contentions that might be otherwise defended but are not advanced here); that instances of Genocide-Denial often stem from ideological rather than historical assumptions seems clear, but also the issue of that genealogy is a subject for a different discussion. The boundaries of the narrower historiographic approach followed here are the more difficult to sustain because many horrific atrocities have been committed and deserve full attention that are nonetheless clearly not genocidal; asserting that about such genocidal claims in no way denies or minimizes the atrocities that were committed, nor would such clarification be considered here as instances of Genocide-Denial. Additionally, there may well be occurrences for which there is no clear means of settling the question of whether the acts identified, even if the descriptions of those acts are agreed upon, fit the definition of genocide. All the more reason, however, for confronting Denial claims on specifically historical grounds. And again, although the six questions framed here appear on the periphery of the phenomenon of Genocide-Denial, they emphasize certain structural elements and presuppositions of that periphery's center that have often been neglected in the reactions to such Denial.

In this line of reasoning, I focus on certain structural features of Denial, its "thick" meaning rhetorically and epistemically, thus locating the phenomenon in relation to facts, counterfacts, and questions either assumed or ignored in its substructure. Thus I point to the presuppositions underlying such absences and the difference that their inclusion would make in analyzing the position. Identical or similar issues have shaped other historiographic critiques, but they have unusual bearing on the Denial position because of the startling social and cultural implication of that view and its marginal status *as* history. Thus the six questions about Denial compose a view of Denial as *itself* a historical datum, even more substantive than the blind moral insult that Denial is commonly taken to be.

1. Is it an implication of Genocide-Denial, in its varieties, that *if*—counterfactually to the Denial—the alleged genocide *had* occurred, Denial advocates would judge it to have been evil, wrongful: as authentic and large crime *as* genocide?
2. Is the Denial position adequately stated in the exclusionary binary distinction between "Denial," on one hand, and "Acknowledgement" or "Affirmation," on the other?
3. Are advocates of Denial lying? That is, do they believe that what they say is false but affirm it anyway? Or do they genuinely believe their own claims, applying to them the same standards they do for other, less morally charged but also empirical and historical claims?
4. Is Genocide-Denial—as many of the supposed instances of genocide addressed by Denial are *also*

claimed to be—historically unique? That is, without likenesses or analogies in historiographic discourse?

5. Have the issues related to the phenomenon of Denial led to any recognizable scholarly or historiographic advances? If so or not, how do these consequences reflect on the Denial position itself?

And finally,

6. What, after everything else that can be has been said about Genocide-Denial, is to be *done* about it in those instances when it is shown to be historically false? That is—by implication—also admitting the possibility that in some instances, certainly in principle, Denial is a defensible position?

In response:

1. Together or separately, the substantive assertions of Denial for any particular claim of genocide or in the pattern of Denial overall (typically, the exaggerated number of victims; the technical incapacity of the alleged means; the "fog of war" thesis; the supposed absence of any overall genocidal design) do not *entail* the corollary that if what these claims deny *had* occurred, the genocide alleged *would have been* a crime or wrongful—but the Denial position as commonly advocated suggests it. The emotive charge in the various Denial assertions, the intensity of Deniers' rejection of the particular genocide's occurrence, is difficult to understand except on the grounds that their subject was assumed to have moral

and legal significance beyond that of only the historical fact. Admittedly, the intensity often accompanying expressions or rejections of Denial *might* reflect
only a strong commitment to historical accuracy—in
the Denier's terms, a wish to right a historiographic
wrong. But the context of Denial claims typically
make this inference improbable, certainly as an
exclusive motive; the nature of the genocides themselves and the charged rhetoric related to them have
themselves become part of the issues surrounding
Denial claims.

What difference does it make if the counterfactual assertion taken here to be implicit in Denial
were explicitly acknowledged by the "schools" of
Denial? Again, this counterfactual states only that if
the genocide(s) alleged *had* occurred—what Denial
denies—it would have been wrongful. One consequence of outing this premise is to underscore the
distinction between the Deniers who claim that
nothing in the way of genocide—the analogues in
other genocides to the Nazis' "Final Solution"—was
plotted or implemented in the particular instance,
but recognize that it would have been wrongful if it
had been. *And* to register the difference between that
position and another reaction to the charge of genocide that carries an even heavier moral weight than
Denial: acknowledgement that atrocities, perhaps
reaching the level of genocide, did occur, but they
were justifiable in principle as a good in itself or as
legitimate self-defense or as collateral damage. Membership in these two groups to some extent overlaps
(contradictory though the two positions are), but the

conceptual and historical differences between them are evident.

Recognition by Denial advocates of genocide's wrongfulness (*if* it did occur) is important as a central, perhaps the only and almost certainly the first point of agreement between Deniers and their critics. Once acknowledged, that juncture may serve as a bridge between the two in subsequent discussion; at the very least, in conceding the wrong of genocide, Deniers could not then reject at least the *possibility* of the occurrence of the genocide at issue, the denial of which has at times been a prop for the Denial position more generally. The concession that if the genocide in dispute had occurred, it would have been wrong would thus mark initial agreement in a debate that more often breaks down as soon as it begins (*if* it begins).

2. Is there an alternative to the binary choice commonly assumed between Denial on one side and acknowledgement or affirmation on the other? Occasional references to groups in the midspace between the two have appeared, with certain internal divisions noted within the extremes themselves over whether what had occurred—or in extreme cases was at the time occurring—should be understood as genocidal. But no systematic attempt has been made to identify intermediate or middle groups, and there seems good reason for challenging the grip of the binary choice by recognizing the existence of a number of groups in the space *between* Denial and its contradictory.

Recognition of one large group in particular among these starts from the current world population, estimated as approximately seven billion. To ask how many of that seven billion have even *heard* of the "six million" (as a leading instance of genocide) is almost certainly to find that the percentage of those who have heard of it is no larger and perhaps considerably smaller than the percentage of people who have *not*. Indeed, even if the number of those who recognize even the outline of the Nazi genocide against the Jews were larger than its opposite, the latter figure would still be in the billions. (The difficulties with this speculation are as obvious as they are unavoidable. The minimal acquaintance indicated is vague in detail even for those who have it, perhaps limited to knowing that something "bad" had occurred—and what holds in relation to the Holocaust would be more one-sided in relation to other twentieth-century genocides, still more to earlier ones.) The large numbers of "non-knowers" in this group, for whom the genocides noted evoke no recognition at all, ought to be identified not as Deniers and not even as indifferent, but more simply as absent. Members of this group have not known the evidence and turned their backs, they simply have not been aware of it—and the size of this group, impossible to determine precisely, obviously is large. (A slight but telling poll among high school seniors in one US state found that 50 percent of *those* students did not know what the Holocaust was, when it occurred, or who did what to whom in it.)

Then, too, other groups also appear between the extremes of Denial and affirmation. A second intermediate group between Holocaust Deniers and affirmers, for example, includes people who are

familiar with the Holocaust as something more than
a name but for whom its occurrence does not matter
(as warranting a reaction) for a variety of reasons:
because of personal or group hardship that has left no
room for empathy with others' suffering; or because
the present distance from the Holocaust of almost
seventy years blends into a view of the historical past
so filled with war and atrocity that another instance,
however large, adds little as warranting a reaction;
or because, more knowledgeable than others, they
juxtapose the Holocaust to other incidents of genocide in ways that minimize the Holocaust's claims not
only to uniqueness but even extremity, thus merging
with other instances of mass killing all of which are
in principle deplorable, whether categorized as genocide or not. Still another response in this group might
characterize the genocide at issue as a response and
thus justification to a threatened genocide (whether
the threat was real or imaginary). In this group of
nonreactions, the "fog of war" turns into a "fog of history": not Denial, neither absence nor ignorance, but
indifference—a sense that whether in reflecting on
their own histories or on history more broadly, the
respondents here find that the genocide in question
(and perhaps any group of them) might as well *not*
have occurred, and in any event makes no demands
on them.

Consideration should be given under this heading also to a group, already mentioned, who fully
recognize the atrocities committed that lead to
charges of genocide but who object to the designation of "genocide" in itself: denial in this sense of the

concept, not its referent as otherwise described. This is obviously a very different sense of "Denial," but it has had a history of its own extending to the early days of the Genocide Convention, and it has a continuing presence—in effect, a presence by affirming the absence of the concept of genocide. The year 1948 saw the passage both of the Genocide Convention and of the Universal Declaration of Human Rights. Unlike the former, the latter was a nonbinding resolution of principles, but in the present context it is notable for its omission of any reference to the threat of genocide as a violation among the many human rights *against violations* that it identifies (including, for example, the right to "vacations"). Lemkin was himself disturbed by the nearly simultaneous advocacy for the Universal Declaration, on the grounds that it drew attention away from the Genocide Convention; Hersh Lauterpacht, a central figure in postwar international legislation, argued similarly from the other side: that the importance of human rights as such and in general should be given priority, with the crime of genocide subordinate to it. In the event, both formulations were adopted by the UN, but the sense of conflict between the two has survived since, with the search for replacements for "genocide" an indication of that. Thus another albeit very different view that by absorbing genocide in other categories would in effect silence its specific claims.

What consequences follow if indeed Denial and its opposite do not constrain us with their standard binary alternatives but stand instead at the two ends of a spectrum with intermediate points between them like those cited? The increasing number of people in this middle space and the possibility that they might remain there or that some might subsequently move toward Denial are reasons for taking this middle space seriously. The superficially irrelevant positions of ignorance or indifference claim a potentially important place alongside Denial—if not in directly supporting it, doing nothing to counter it as a potential choice and certainly nothing in the present to assess or even to address it in its own demanding terms.

3. To ask if advocates of specific instances of Denial believe their own claims is not as mischievously ad hominem as it might appear, nor does it preclude testing the Deniers' claims in empirically historical terms. Its potential significance, in fact, is much like the analogous question that was directed to the description of the Jews by Nazi racial "science" as a "cancer" or "bacillus"—thus, as a literal biological threat. Some Nazi adherents undoubtedly believed these claims, and on that basis, the "Final Solution" could be rationalized as self-defense. But many important Nazis in the hierarchy, like many non-Party Germans, are known to have been skeptical, paying no more than lip service to the scientific or medical "threat." Other inconsistencies and differences appear among the advocates of Denial, including such nonideological or nonprincipled motives as economic self-interest and peer pressure, both of which have been shown to have impinged on most if not all the alleged genocides cited. Such ad hominem criticism is not by itself disproof of Denial's historical

or other evidentiary claims, but it is not irrelevant to their assessment.

And then, too, the motives of Genocide-Deniers matter most immediately if we view differently those who act on what they believe to be true (even if mistakenly) from those who act (perhaps in the same way) on what they recognize as false but nonetheless profess to be true: a difference, in other words, between Deniers speaking "in good faith" (odd as that locution is) and those who lie their way to the same conclusions and actions. The question of "Why Denial *at all?*" is relevant to both sides of this distinction, although (again on both sides) it is bottomless through its questioning of a refurbished formula for other commonplace prejudices. In the end, it evokes the still broader question of "Why *prejudice?*"—greatly magnified as the prejudice becomes a basis not only for social discrimination but for group-murder.

4. Is Genocide-Denial unique in the chronicles of pure or applied historiography? As soon as the question is put, the answer is obvious: "No, certainly not. Not unique, not unprecedented, arguably not even the most flagrant among examples of atrocity denial." Another egregious instance of atrocity denial also emerged from World War II—in the systemic Japanese atrocities committed in China, including but extending beyond the Rape of Nanking. In one respect, moreover, the pattern of the Japanese denial of those atrocities has been more extreme than Genocide-Denial in relation to the Nazis, since the former was sustained by the concurrence of

certain postwar Japanese governments: in effect, Denial with official sanction. This notable instance of Denial joins numerous others, long-standing or recent, which employ virtually the same tactics as Holocaust-Denial: disputing the numbers of victim; tu quoques, quasi justifications by citing the threat of internal subversion; arguments from self-defense; and, often, appeals to the comforting fogs of war. (In the last of these, the context of war that has often provided a cover for genocide itself serves also, retroactively, as a cover for its denial.)

The "genre" of Denial that surfaces in this way does not imply equivalence among its instances, but it does suggest a common trope that figures the space between atrocity and its historical narratives. That trope was extended in post–World War II political rhetoric as a general linguistic trope by the subtler concept of "denia*bility*": a tactic relying on unverifiability that goes a step beyond outright Denial in the sense that it is often, if not always, nonfalsifiable. A paradigm of nonfalsifiable deniability is the first-person claim that "I have no memory of such and such events." These varieties in the expression and scope of historical denial suggest a need for a conceptual "anatomy" of Denial to sort through the tissue of Denial motives, means, and uses. Denial might well emerge here not as an occasionally deviant narrative but as a historiographic category, suggesting—and not only on this ground—the need for a General Theory of Historical Denial.

5. Has any good or benefit emerged as a consequence of Genocide-Denial—for understanding the

phenomenon of Denial or for analyzing the character of genocide itself? This delicate question should
be distinguished from the cliché—a shaky claim in a
shakier philosophy of history—that finds a silver lin-
ing in every cloud. No such implication follows from
what has been said here, but quite aside from that,
the question warrants consideration in reflecting
on the history of the study of genocide. The near
consensus now on many dates, facts, and numbers
relevant to specific alleged instances of genocides
might not differ *radically* if Deniers' claims had not
been raised and confronted, but the impetus for
certain historical investigations has clearly come
partly in response to Denial claims. So, for example,
the doubt raised by instances of Holocaust-Denial of
whether the gas chambers in the death camps that
used them *could have* killed the numbers of victims
alleged has been an immediate source for testing the
dimensions of the gas chambers and the gassing process itself. So, too, the cumulative evidence of orders
discovered as sent from the central Turkish government concerning the expulsion and annihilation of
the Armenian populace. To be sure, measuring the
capacity of the gas chambers of Auschwitz could
have and probably would have been accomplished
without the Deniers' challenge—but probably not
as soon or as fully as it was; and the same dialectic
holds in relation to the issue of Turkish government
involvement in the massacre of Turkish Armenians.
There is no more reason to dispute this than to doubt
that far from supporting the Denial position, the
information gathered in this way has only further

undermined its claims: a variation on "poetic justice" in the bulkier shape of "historiographic justice."

6. What, now and after all, can be *done* about Genocide-Denial and the uses to which it has been or may yet be put—where, as has been shown, the historical evidence and corresponding moral outrage are disproportionately large? This familiar question propels the past into the present where practical judgment can no longer find refuge in retrospective speculation. What, *specifically*, is to be done? Admittedly, the uses to which Denial has been put in its most egregiously problematic cases has built on independent origins and motives: antisemitism and anti-Zionism, for example, did not wait for the Nazi genocide to find *their* rationale—nor did German or other expressions of nationalism that have at times also deployed versions of Denial for support. But these convergent sources only underscore the importance of facing the phenomenon of Denial in its recurrent and menacing presence.

Two examples related to Holocaust-Denial may point to the difficulties involved in confronting the phenomenon of Denial more generally. At Northwestern University in 1989, in the first of what then became the biannual Lessons and Legacies conferences on the Holocaust, Saul Friedländer delivered a plenary address to an audience that included conference participants, university faculty and students, and the public. Following his lecture, Friedländer responded to questions from the audience—until one question was asked to which he began to respond but then stopped: Peter Hayes, the session chair, had said something to Friedländer who then interrupted his response with words to this effect: "Professor Butz, because of what you have written about the matters we are discussing, I decline to respond to your question." The person who had asked the question subsided with only a rustle of protest. He was Arthur Butz, a professor of engineering at Northwestern and the author of *The Hoax of the Twentieth Century*. And here a question arises that persists twenty-five years later. Friedländer's lecture, although part of the Conference program, was open to the public and was presented in a university building; the person asking the question was a university faculty member. Not everyone in the audience was affiliated with the university, but there was common understanding that anyone present could participate in the discussion after the lecture. In these terms, Friedländer's refusal to respond to Butz's question becomes itself a question. For even putting aside the consideration that this exchange took place in an academic setting, the question was framed here of how (or whether) Genocide-Denial is to be confronted. Is the issue to be decided on the basis of personal moral intuitions or decisions? Should there be legal regulations governing the expressions?

A second formulation raises this specific occurrence to a more general level. Deborah Lipstadt who in *Denying the Holocaust* brought the Denial issue to broad public attention (and who was later the victorious defendant in the David Irving trial in Great Britain after he sued her for libel in charging *him* with Denial), had stated earlier that she would not appear on the same platform (lecture, panel, television or radio) with Deniers. To do so, she held, would represent their position as a respectable, or at least debatable, historical view—a claim she rejected. So far as I know, Lipstadt has not argued that Deniers should be banned from speaking on university campuses or elsewhere, and she has explicitly opposed legislative measures criminalizing or otherwise penalizing expressions of Holocaust-Denial. Nonetheless, in the course of her writing and speaking as she built her rebuttal of the Denial view, Lipstadt provides detailed and full accounts of that view—as how could she not? (So far as I am aware, Friedländer does not in his writings address Holocaust-Denial as such, although his work on the history of the Holocaust clearly amounts to a rebuttal.)

Here, in any event, the question of "What is to be done?" about Denial becomes more complex. Lipstadt's own position in her writings which address the specific assertions of Denial and the "evidence" they draw on differs in its medium from a personal confrontation or sharing a lecture platform with Deniers, but it nonetheless constitutes recognition of the Denial position; indeed, she provides in her writing a fuller representation of the position than any single Denier has done. (Her live encounter with Irving in a court of law is a different though not unrelated matter.) And in fact, writing involves many of the same modes of moral and legal address that oral argument does: always there is an "implied reader" or "implied listener," irrespective of whether that person is physically present or not; always there is the effort to parse and counter the structure of an argument: evidence, premises, conclusions—and the relations among them. The systematic issue at stake here thus comes into clearer view: what form or medium *should* responses to Holocaust-Denial or, in its more general form, Genocide-Denial take?

If face-to-face encounters are admissible, then Friedländer was wrong to rule Butz's question out of order—as Lipstadt's view would be faulty at a more general level. Should responses come only in *written* disputation? The latter practice has, of course, been common—whether explicitly aimed at Deniers or in broader analyses that counter Deniers' claims.

Should *legislative* measures, criminal or civil, be adopted as a means of prevention or punishment? Even legislation to this effect would not settle the primarily moral question of whether anyone in the jurisdiction should engage in live confrontations with Deniers (the courtroom, in such an eventuality, would seem a neutral exception). One clear consequence of this option, however, would be (has been) its political, moral, and economic liabilities. Minimally, it faces the intrinsic problem of all prohibitions: that their articulation of whatever they proscribe brings it into fuller view than would otherwise occur. Furthermore, the economic costs for the legal, juridical, and practical measures required to enforce the legislation are predictable. Beyond these practical issues, furthermore, are two weighty issues of principle: the implications of this legislation for the principle of free speech and the role that the legislation assigns the judiciary of determining and enforcing a specific historical finding. (Courts deal as a matter of course with the "finding" of facts—but rarely with the "facts" of large-scale historical events and, except in cases of libel or slander, virtually never in imposing penalties for the denial or misrepresentation of such findings). Then, too, in considering the consequences of such legislation for the public face of the Denial view itself, the question persists of whether such legislation would indeed reduce or even hinder expressions of Denial. What practical influence of *any* kind would it have? The lengthy history of censorship has yielded mixed—and often, unknown—results in relation to the occurrence of whatever is being censored.

Versions of the legislative option have indeed been adopted by fourteen countries, in laws that in effect proscribe Denial, whether by prohibiting "genocide denial" generally or specifically naming an instance of genocide (the Holocaust, for example) as "undeniable" or by broader laws banning group hate speech or libel which are understood to include instances of Genocide-Denial. Countries as culturally different as Canada and Israel, Australia and Germany, Sweden and France, Switzerland and New Zealand have adopted versions of such laws; several of these countries have initiated prosecutions based on them. But the two principal questions for assessing legislation to this effect persist: First, what are its likely (or once implemented, actual) consequences? Does the legislations in fact deter? Is its obvious symbolic, beyond its practical function, effective? And second, what are the *costs* of implementing such measures, material but also symbolic and in principle? Do the benefits (e.g., of deterrence, if that were demonstrated) outweigh such liabilities as the encroachment on freedom of expression?

The first of these questions remains unanswered, perhaps unanswerable—suggesting that deterrence is probably not the legislation's primary goal. (The deterrent effect of other "standard" punishments, including capital punishment, also remains in dispute—perhaps pointing to the same conclusion.) Much, however, *is* known about the costs of the legislation. The material costs, in court action and enforcement, are formidable if the laws are applied consistently. The related symbolic effect seems bound to cut both ways—on one hand stigmatizing the views against which the laws are directed, but on the other hand imposing another, conceptually vague limit on free expression. Enforcement itself poses problems, as became only too evident in the guilty verdict of a French court against the historian Bernard Lewis (discussed in chapter 3) for his "denial" of Turkey's attacks on its Armenian populace in 1915–17 as genocide. The symbolic fine of one franc imposed on Lewis in conjunction with the judge's equivocal rationale for the verdict of guilt arguably diminished whatever weight the trial might otherwise have had. And then, too, bridging these two sets of issues is another that combines epistemic and legal elements—namely, the assumption that a court of law is in a position to determine the "correct" narrative of a complex historical event and then to impose legal penalties on the basis of that determination.

Few even of the most outspoken defenders of free speech have argued that there should be *no* limits to that freedom. Libel or slander, the incitement to riot, and also the more marginal case of "fighting words" have been accepted as reasonable if contestable limitations. To extend these exceptional categories to include statements about particular historical events claimed not only to be false (on that charge, the number of trials warranted would be endless and hopeless), but also to be false *and* offensive to a group sensibility or dignity strains those boundaries still further. On Justice Holmes's much cited example, for someone to shout "Fire" (knowing there is none) in a crowded theater is immediately life threatening and legitimately charged as criminal. But that example involves a significantly greater disproportion between speech and consequence than figures in verbal or written Genocide-Denial and the "offense" or "insult" or "trivialization" it effects, however substantial the counterevidence. Unfortunate as it is, demeaning or offensive words are not an uncommon feature of everyday experience without being subject to legal sanction (whether that judgment of the words challenged is warranted is a separate issue). But the legislation passed in relation to the category of "hate speech," although applicable at times to attacks on individuals, has a broader primary target. As genocide involves group-murder, so the instances covered by hate speech legislation have been directed against *group* hate speech. And however convincing *that* distinction is, the question of whether legislation directed against the level of collective or group hate speech is warranted persists—in good measure because of the strong evidence of its liabilities.

The possibilities considered may not seem to advance the question of what *should* be done about Genocide-Denial. In considering the two responses of oral or written critique, it might be argued that they propose too little—as the third response of imposing civil or criminal sanctions proposes too much. A fourth option of simply ignoring the claims of Genocide-Deniers has attractions beyond its simplicity, since at least in the long run instances of Genocide-Denial (as seems to have occurred for Holocaust-Denial) may fall of their own weight, professed finally by only a small group no more credible than the Flat Earth Society. Certainly, compared to other historical questions related to the phenomenon of genocide in general or in its specific appearances that continue to require research and analysis—including the most basic question of what causal factors led to specific instances of genocide—the political and moral issues raised by the advocates of Denial seem less urgent and probably less enduring. Historians who in their work labor to analyze and to detail the process of genocide are in effect opposing Genocide-Denial even when they do not directly confront that view in its specific claims—but that indirection may seem still less than the false charge of Genocide-Denial, when that occurs, warrants.

Finally, it is also possible that the question of, "What is to be done about Genocide-Denial?" may not call for a general solution at all, but for a nest of individual responses linked together by a common grasp of fact and moral understanding. Some such management seems to have figured in the response of certain non-Germans who, almost seventy years after the Holocaust and despite Germany's efforts of acknowledgement and "Wiedergutmachung" ("reparations") still refuse to visit the country or to buy its products. This has not amounted to a call for a general boycott, but remains a form of individual expression, largely symbolic, and also itself evolving (often diminishing). Analogously, the choice between responding to Holocaust-Denial through writing or by oral address is arguably also a matter for personal, "local" judgment rather than a general rule. Criminal and civil laws are obviously more than only personal expressions, but the objections to them that have been cited arguably outweigh whatever benefits they might bring.

It might be objected that all these alternatives focus exclusively on public discourse or rhetoric and to that

extent ignore the potential role of civil programs or policies that might counter Genocide-Denial more effectively,
as, for example, through systems or programs of public
education. But public discourse is where initiatives for
public or civic action originate, and here again one can
only repeat the obvious: a minimal condition for confronting Genocide-Denial is through the light shed by
evidence and argument, including a search for the roots
and patterns of instances of such Denial. To trace these,
with the conclusions drawn then serving as a base for
broader theoretical and imaginative representations, is
precisely the work that historians in general and historians of human rights in particular have undertaken and it
remains the key to any analysis of Genocide-Denial and of
the possible responses to it.

There will undoubtedly also continue to be disagreement on whether, even if it were *possible* to silence expressions of Genocide-Denial, that course of action should be
adopted. However one judges John Stuart Mill's claim in
On Liberty that false positions have the value of testing,
thus of strengthening whatever we take to be true—and
therefore that false positions should be voiced (perhaps
encouraged?) even if they *could be* silenced—this seems
hardly relevant for Genocide-Denial that does not, even
in the most egregious instances of genocide, lack for advocates. Given the public presence of Genocide-Denial, it is
the more evident that confidence in assessing it depends
mainly on its claims being confronted rather than either
ignored or punished—a line of argument that indeed
echoes the Mill-like premise that censorship is at least as
likely to achieve the opposite of its goals as the goals it
hopes to realize.

Even this restraint, however, would leave room for exceptions, recognizing that Genocide-Denial often has a more presumptive presence than other historical claims. To grant a special historical or moral place (i.e., stigma) for Genocide- or Holocaust-Denial in the public discourse of Germany or Israel, for instance, still leaves a range of options even in those settings. So, for example, legislative measures criminalizing Denial in some form might attach to them a "sunset" clause—as it must be clear that for any such legislation, time is likely to erode current urgencies; legislation is always set, deliberately or not, in the context of history and its contingencies.

***

A concluding comment must unfortunately be attached here about misuses of the charge of Genocide-Denial itself. For just as accounts of specific acts of genocide have been misrepresented in political, artistic, and even historical discourse—as in exaggerated applications of "genocide" or "Nazi" to occurrences or persons essentially dissimilar from their originals—so the charge of Genocide-Denial has also come to be used as a term of opprobrium for avoidance or silence about recognizable atrocities or even lesser occurrences that are, in any event, *not* genocidal. The emphasis in these pages on identifying the specific character of genocide has attempted to show how the charge of "genocide" may itself be open to abuse, either unconsciously or willfully, in its application to atrocities which, however horrific, are clearly not genocidal. And so also the charge of "Genocide-Denial" has come to be applied with a broad brush for efforts related to much lesser acts, either to events that are not genocide (and are alleged not to be) or even to events which are genocide but are questioned on particular issues (e.g., on whether particular records should be made public or not). When an official at a national Holocaust museum charges the director of a German archive with Holocaust-Denial for refusing to release certain data, one sees a gesture in this direction (however warranted the request for the data was). Similarly, when "post-Zionist" historians are labeled Holocaust-Deniers because of their criticism of the received narrative of Israeli history that places an idealized Zionism (and "negation of the Diaspora") at its center, one sees another version of historical and not only metaphorical misprision. Like Holocaust-Denial itself, there is no plausible means of preventing such abuse, but a necessary response is possible in demonstrating, time and time again if necessary, how such figurative expressions or analogies overstate, skew, and, finally, undermine the position they profess to defend. Again, Genocide-Denial is not only a matter of words, but its public presence and practical consequences make their mark *through* words. And if, as I have been claiming, to impose legal limits on what is permissibly said about instances of genocide exacts a greater cost than the good it might accomplish, this yet leaves a wide range of options—in the power of *other* words to undo and then go beyond the Deniers' Denial.

After Words

The discussion here has revolved around three claims that I hope to have made clear and persuasive. First, that the term and concept, "genocide," have justifiably achieved a normative place in current legal, moral, and popular discourse based on its identification of the crime of group-murder. Second, that objections that have been raised to elements of the term and concept, "genocide," can be largely accommodated within the reach of "genocide" itself—by the precedents accumulated in international legal action and by conceptual clarification or amendment to the Genocide Convention itself. And third, that the alternative terms and concepts to "genocide" proposed by its critics as replacements for it seem to suffer from the same or other faults than those ascribed to it; more importantly, they fail to give adequate account of the specific crime that "genocide" defined. Thus they would leave that atrocity the nameless crime it had been before the concept's appearance.

There may be other evidence and arguments than what I have given here to support these claims, as there may also be counterevidence or counterarguments that I have failed to take into account. But these possibilities only underscore the fact that "genocide" has to take its chances in the conceptual and empirical world in the same way that the act of genocide established *its* historical presence, impelled by varied but intelligible patterns of causality. In the end, it is the claim about genocide as a distinctive moral violation in the already harsh friction of the commonplace world to which reflection on events grouped and addressed in the charge of genocide must answer. The twentieth century provided more grist for such reflection than had previously been thought possible; one has only to consider the optimistic views in 1915 on both sides of the "Great War"—that "war to end all wars"—to recognize that history has a body as well as a mind of its own. Subterraneously, the ground was being laid for a full century in which genocide, not in its first appearances but in its most systematically realized acts, was to become a familiar feature in the historical landscape.

Was this the most consequential development in that century? The competition is strong, and certainly the related phenomenon of "industrial killing"—as in mass murder, from which I have claimed genocide must be distinguished—would itself have a notable claim. Yet there is also another side to what thus appears as a "progressive" view of the history of wrongdoing or evil. Lest the balance be conceded too quickly to a view here of the moral imagination as linked disproportionately to acts of wrongdoing, one would have also to recognize that the ideal of an international community bound by and to international law, previously so remote practically as to seem utopian, gained traction during that century to an unprecedented extent. Was this truly *moral* progress? Of course, technological advances in communication and transportation, related only obliquely to ethical judgment, contributed to this moral and political "development," but no more than had been required for the flourishing of the authoritarian state and *its* genocidal tendencies. By the time the Nazi genocide against the Jews reached its full scale, the instruments required for its implementation already qualified as "low-tech"; in a retrospective view from 2016, this seems increasingly likely to hold for future genocides as well. Genocide is now more easily imagined, planned, and implemented than ever before—making it still more urgent that the moral imagination required to *counter* it should keep pace. If present international legislation and systems of judgment are yet inadequate, it becomes the more pressing that they should be strengthened, not discarded and not replaced by others that repeat the flaws alleged in their predecessors. International legislation and judicial rulings through the United Nations and the International Criminal Court represent notable commitments to standards binding the world's nations and their inhabitants. When the Genocide Convention aimed at the "Prevention and Punishment of the Crime of Genocide," what was clearly needed was not only a conceptual structure for *identifying* genocide but also a means for "preventing and punishing" of the crime. The Genocide Convention itself provided a model for the step of identification, and the seventy years of its history since have seen important steps toward that definition's general acceptance. Steps have also been taken, slowly and even hesitantly, toward realizing the second phase of what the Convention mandated: prevention (and, one might add, intervention) and punishment. Actions toward those ends remain the largest current challenge posed by the phenomenon of genocide; however common and forceful the recognition of that phenomenon's past is, it is obviously insufficient by itself for anticipating or preventing its future.

The moral principle at stake here is straightforward: as group-identity becomes increasingly fragile, threatened externally and internally by cross- and transcultural currents in both wartime and in peace, it becomes increasingly pressing—culturally, politically, morally—that the concept of the *social* self be recognized, a self which is not only a member of communities but dependent on that membership—dependent for *its* existence on theirs, at times on a dominant single group but even then also on a confluence of others—and that practical steps are needed to sustain that balance. This is not an argument against the possibility or desirability of a single world community or government that might, for better or worse, supersede the present variety of smaller-scale communities, and one might doubt that any such comprehensive structure could provide the concrete particularity, the binding sense of difference integral in smaller and partial social bodies. At any rate, that issue is not the most compelling one among the pressures on the contemporary world, certainly not in comparison to the present and widespread threat to communities doing the work of sustaining the social— *and* individual—lives of their members. The *need* for such communities and such work remains a compelling basis for the "defense of 'genocide'"; the need for that defense is driven by the past and the likely future of genocide itself.

Bibliographical Notes

Chapter 1

On the historical conceptualization of evil, see Susan Neiman, *Evil in Modern Thought: An Alternative History of Philosophy* (Princeton, NJ: Princeton University Press, 2002); Luke Russell, *Evil: A Philosophical Investigation* (New York: Oxford University Press, 2014); Richard J. Bernstein, *Radical Evil: A Philosophical Interrogation* (Cambridge, UK: Blackwells, 2002); Reinhold Niebuhr, *Moral Man and Immoral Society* (London: SCM Press, 1963). Stephen Pinker, *The Better Angels of Our Nature: Why Violence Has Declined* (New York: Viking, 2011), finds a linear progression historically *away* from evil with twentieth- and twenty-first-century genocides insufficient as counterevidence.

On moral history and theory in relation to genocide and *its* history, see Raphael Lemkin, *Axis Rule in Occupied Europe* (Washington, DC: Carnegie Endowment for International Peace, 1944); William A. Schabas, *Genocide in International Law: The Crime of Crimes* (Cambridge, UK: Cambridge University Press, 2000); Mark Levene, *Genocide in the Age of the Nation-State*

(New York: Palgrave Macmillan, 2005); Berel Lang, *Act and Idea in the Nazi Genocide* (Chicago: University of Chicago Press, 1990). Timothy Snyder, *Bloodlands* (New York: Basic Books, 2010) gives an account of modern atrocities in Eastern Europe but significantly avoiding nearly all reference to genocide; his *Black Earth: The Holocaust as History and Warning* (New York: Penguin Random House, 2015), although emphasizing Hitler's responsibility for the Nazi genocide, minimizes the relevance of genocide as a general phenomenon.

On the concept of intention, see Elisabeth Anscombe, *Intentions* (Ithaca, NY: Cornell University Press, 1957) and *Essays on Anscombe's Intention*, eds. Anton Ford, Jennifer Horsby, Frederick Startland (Cambridge, MA: Harvard University Press, 2011). For discussion of corporate in relation to individual intentions, see Peter French, "The Corporation as a Moral Person," in *American Philosophical Quarterly*, 16:3 (1979); Margaret Gilbert, *A Theory of Political Obligation* (Oxford: Oxford University Press, 2006); Christian List and Philip Petit, *Group Agency: The Possibility, Design, and Status of Corporate Agents* (Oxford: Oxford University Press, 2011).

For the history of conceptual and legal development of natural rights theory, see Richard Tuck, *Natural Rights Theory* (Cambridge, UK: Cambridge University Press, 1976); C. B. Macpherson, *The Political Theory of Possessive Individualism: Hobbes to Locke* (Oxford: Clarendon Press, 1962); A. John Simons, *The Lockean Theory of Rights* (Princeton, NJ: Princeton University Press, 1992).

Chapter 2

On Draco and draconian punishment, see Edwin Cara-
wan, *Rhetoric and the Law of Draco* (New Haven, CT:
Yale University Press, 1981). On issues of comparative
evil, the various accounts of the utilitarian calculus
have been the most sustained attempt to place morally relevant acts in a single table of measurement—
with its classic formulation in Bentham's "hedonic
calculus," see Jeremy Bentham *An Introduction to the
Principles of Morals and Legislation* (Oxford: Clarendon Press, 1907); Jeremy Waldron, ed., *Nonsense
upon Stilts* (London: Methuen, 1987). For a recent
formulations of that view, see Peter Singer, *Writings
on an Ethical Life* (New York: Harper Collins, 2000);
for criticism, see Bernard Williams, "A Critique of
Utilitarianism," in J. J. C. Smart and Bernard Williams, eds., *Utilitarianism: For and Against* (Cambridge, UK: Cambridge University Press, 1973); David
Lagons, "The Moral Opacity of Utilitarianism," in
Elinor Mason and Dale Miller, eds., *Morality, Rules,
and Consequences* (New York: Rowman & Littlefield,
2000). On specific comparisons between or among
recent atrocities, including acts of genocide, see Levon
Chorbajian and George Shirunian, eds., *Studies in
Comparative Genocide* (New York: St. Martin's, 1999).

Chapter 3

The two books at the focus of this chapter raise issues
bearing on the concept of genocide in general: Marc

Nichanian, *The Historiographic Perversion* (New York: Columbia University Press, 2010) and Larry May, *Genocide: A Normative Account* (Cambridge, UK: Cambridge University Press, 2010). May amplifies the views noted here elsewhere; see *After War Ends* (New York: Cambridge University Press, 2012); Larry May and Zachary Hoskins, eds., *International Criminal Law and Philosophy* (New York: Cambridge University Press, 2010). At the same time that May claims that "collectivities and other abstract names are fictions in that they do not have a referent in the existing universe," he argues also against individual responsibility for corporate or group atrocities—claiming in other words, that "collectivities" are real enough to commit but not to suffer genocide.

Both the "uniqueness" question raised by Nichanian and May's "nominalist" critique of group-identity have recurred in the history of the concept of genocide. As mentioned, May's nominalism seems to rule out even the logical possibility of genocide. The "uniqueness" thesis that Nichanian advances in relation to the Armenian Aghed has appeared often in other contexts as well, most widely in references to the Nazi genocide against the Jews, as in Yehuda Bauer's claim that the Holocaust warrants a category independent of—*beyond*—genocide. Bauer later modified this view although still emphasizing the Holocaust's *distinctive* features. (On the evolution in Bauer's thinking, see his *The Holocaust in Historical Perspective* [Seattle: University of Washington Press, 1978] and *Rethinking the Holocaust* [New Haven, CT: Yale University Press, 2001].) Both "uniqueness" and "distinctive" have been repeatedly applied (at times as synonyms) to the Holocaust; the same conflation has appeared in relation to other genocides and to atrocities that do not meet the criteria of genocide (as in references to the Palestinian "Naqba" ["the Catastrophe"]). In the history of the people affected, the historical event thus singled out may be unique; in the wider historical framework, however, the difference between "uniqueness" and "distinctiveness" becomes more telling. See further on this question Alan S. Rosenbaum, ed., *Is the Holocaust Unique? Perspectives on Comparative Genocide* (Boulder, CO: Westview Press, 2009); Dan Stone, "The Historiography of Genocide: Beyond 'Uniqueness' and Ethnic Superstition," in *Rethinking History*, 8:1 (2009). For sources on group-rights and its presupposition of the *reality* of groups, see references below in chapter 7.

Chapter 4

Systematic and general issues related to the concept of genocide are raised by Boghossian in his essay "The Concept of Genocide," published together with his response to reactions to his analysis by Berel Lang, Eric Weitz, and William R. Schabas in the *Journal of Genocide Studies*, 12 (2010). Schabas's own more extensive (and conflicting) advocacy on behalf of the term and concept "genocide" appears in his *Genocide in International Law: The Crime of Crimes*. For other conceptual analyses, in addition to May's *Genocide: A Normative Account*, see Joyce Apsel and Ernesto Verdija, *Genocide Matters: Ongoing Issues and*

Emerging Perspectives (New York: Routledge, 2013); Claudia Card, *Confronting Evil: Terrorism, Torture, Genocide* (New York: Cambridge University Press, 2010); Rene Provost and Pagam Akhavan, eds., *Confronting Genocide* (New York: Springer, 2011). On issues related to the prevention of genocide (or the possibility of intervention in it), see Daniel Chirot and Clark McCauley, *Why Not Kill Them All?* (Princeton, NJ: Princeton University Press, 2006); also publications of the United States' Atrocity Prevention Board, the Early Warning Project of the United States Holocaust Memorial Museum, and Genocide Watch.

Chapter 5

Conflicting attributions that are unlikely to be resolved have been claimed for the earliest use—the *authorship*—of "Holocaust" as designating the Nazi genocide; conceptual questions about the continuing use of the term itself can still be directly addressed, especially in relation to the spread of alternative terms like "Shoah" or the attachment of a particular qualifier ("Nazi" or "German" or otherwise, "Jewish") to "Genocide." For analyses of Nazi language, see Victor Klemperer's study, *The Language of the Third Reich: LTI, Lingui Tertii Imperii; A Philologist's Notebook*, trans. Martin Brady (New Brunswick, NJ: Athlone Press, 2000); Jean-Pierre Faye, *Languages totalitaires* (Paris: Hermann, 2004); Berel Lang, "Intending Genocide," in *Act and Idea in the Nazi Genocide*, (Chicago: University of Chicago Press, 1990).

Chapter 6

On Lemkin's life in relation to the Genocide Convention, see his unfinished autobiography, *Totally Unofficial: The Autobiography of Raphael Lemkin*, ed. Donna Lee-Frieze (New Haven, CT: Yale University Press, 2013). For fuller accounts, see Samantha Power, *"A Problem from Hell": America in the Age of Genocide* (New York: Basic Books, 2002); John Cooper, *Raphael Lemkin and the Struggle for the Genocide Convention* (New York: Palgrave Macmillan, 2008); Douglas Irvin-Erickson, *Raphael Lemkin and Genocide: A Political History of Genocide in Theory and Law* (Philadelphia: University of Pennsylvania Press, 2016); Philippe Sands, *East West Street: On the Origins of "Genocide" and "Crimes Against Humanity"* (London: Alfred Knopf & Weidenfeld, 2016); Annette Becker, "Penser et nommer les génocides: Raphael Lemkin" (privately circulated). Other relevant texts are Steven Jacobs, *Raphael Lemkin's Thoughts on Nazi Genocide: Not Guilty?* (Lewiston: E. Mellon Press, 1992); William Korey, *An Epitaph for Raphael Lemkin* (New York: Jacob Blaustein Institute for the Advancement of Human Rights, 2001); Nehemiah Robinson: *The Genocide Convention: Its Origin and Interpretation* (New York: World Jewish Congress, 1949).

Chapter 7

On the history of the relation between natural and human rights, see Samuel Moyn, *The Last Utopia:*

Human Rights in History (Cambridge, MA: Harvard University Press, 2010) and *Human Rights and the Uses of History* (London: Verso Books, 2014). Moyn agrees on the traditional status of natural rights as individualist—but adds the claim that, historically, those rights were linked invariably, even essentially, to the role of citizenship. Asserting that linkage ascribes a systematic inconsistency to the concept of natural rights that seems absent from classic formulations of that doctrine, like John Locke's *Second Treatise on Civil Government*; the (alleged) connection also undergirds Moyn's account of the history of the human rights movement as originating in the internationalist and post–World War II emphasis of human rights doctrine (versus the earlier nationalist emphasis); it thus obscures if it does not directly deny the continuous historical relationship in the transition from formulations of natural rights to those of human rights. Lynn Hunt's more sustained historical analysis (*Inventing Human Rights: A History* [New York: W. W. Norton, 2007]) notes an intriguing shift in Thomas Jefferson's language from "natural rights" to "human rights" after 1789 (presumably in response to the French Declaration on the Rights of Man and Citizen). She does not, however, place weight on the shift then or more generally; the substantive difference between the two phrases is arguable, although one means of pointing it seems evident in the 1948 United Nations Universal Declaration of Human Rights. Article 15 of the Declaration refers to everyone's—presumably human—"right to a nationality" and Article 24, to a "right to rest and leisure . . . including periodic holidays with pay," both

those rights so clearly tied to social circumstance as
to make equating them with "natural" or inalienable
claims problematic.

On the history of minority and group-rights, see Patrick
Thornbery, *International Law and the Rights of Minorities* (Oxford: Oxford University Press, 1991). For issues
and references bearing specifically on the concept of
group-rights, also for that concept's historical evolu-
tion, see Will Kymlicka, *A Liberal Theory of Minority
Rights* (Oxford: Oxford University Press, 1995); Will
Kymlicka, ed., *The Rights of Minority Cultures* (Oxford:
Oxford University Press, 1995); Judith Baker, ed.,
Group Rights (Toronto: University of Toronto Press,
1994). On potential conflicts between individual
rights and group-rights, see Avigail Eisenberg and
Jeff Spinner-Halev, eds., *Minorities within Minorities*
(Cambridge, UK: Cambridge University Press, 2005);
Jeremy Waldron, "Taking Group Rights Carefully," in
G. Huscroft and P. Rishworth, eds., *Litigating Rights:
Perspectives from Domestic and International Law*
(Oxford: Hart, 2002). On the "right to exit" in relation
to the status of groups, see David Gauthier, "Breaking-
Up: An Essay on Secession," in *Canadian Journal of
Philosophy*, 24:3 (1994): 357–72.

Edward Luttwak's comments on the Genocide Convention appeared in the *London Review of Books*, 37:11
(2015).

Chapter 8

Hannah Arendt's *Eichmann in Jerusalem: A Report on the Banality of Evil* appeared first in three issues of the *New Yorker*, beginning with the February 16, 1963 issue; it was published in book form later in the year by Viking Press (New York) and then in a revised edition (from which the citations here are taken) in 1965 with a postscript added by Arendt and certain other changes. The continuing criticism of Arendt's account has focused mainly on two points: Arendt's contention that the Jewish communities in Nazi-occupied countries, principally through the Jewish councils (Judenräte), were complicit in the communities' destruction, responsible for more deaths than would have occurred without the work of such organizations; and second—the issue addressed here—that the "banality of evil" thesis does not withstand scrutiny, whether as a description of evil as such or as applied to Eichmann. In relation to the charge of communal responsibility, the balance of historical opinion has been heavily against Arendt's position, although not always on the same grounds. On the "banality" thesis, recent discussions, drawing on records reexamined or newly brought to light, have argued for Eichmann's strong—and deep, nonbanal—commitment to Nazism. See, along these lines, David Cesarani, *Becoming Eichmann: Rethinking the Life, Crimes and Trial of a Mass Murderer* (New York: Da Capo, 2006); Deborah Lipstadt, *The Eichmann Trial* (New York: Schocken, 2011); Bettina Stangneth, *Eichmann before Jerusalem: The Unexamined Life of a Mass Murderer*, trans. Ruth Martin (New York: Knopf,

2014). For a defense of Arendt's "banality" thesis that finds it a revision rather than a rejection of radical evil, see Richard Bernstein, *Hannah Arendt and the Jewish Question* (Cambridge, MA: MIT Press, 1996). Arendt's "Eichmann" is based on her experience of the Jerusalem trial which began on April 11, 1961 and the records introduced there; whether she would have altered her view of Eichmann's "banality" on the basis of the records unavailable to her at the time is an open question. My account here is a qualified defense of her view of Eichmann even taking into account that additional documentation.

Chapter 9

For a representative formulation of Holocaust-Denial, see Arthur R. Butz, *The Hoax of the Twentieth Century: The Case against the Presumed Extermination of European Jewry* (Los Angeles: Noonday Press, 1976); see also issues of the *Journal of Historical Review* published (1980–92) by the Institute for Historical Review, Torrance, CA. Denial of wartime or other atrocities not identified as genocide is commonplace, often with elements of the Genocide-Denial arguments cited here; for Genocide-Denial claims (and their counterarguments), the determination of corporate intention, a necessary condition of genocide, is a persistent issue. For reactions to Holocaust-Denial as a principal instance of Genocide-Denial, see Deborah Lipstadt, *Denying the Holocaust: The Growing Assault on Truth and Memory* (New York: Free Press, 1993); *History on Trial: My Day in Court with David Irving* (New York: Ecco, 2005). See also Stephen E. Atkins, *Holocaust Denial as an International Movement* (Westport, CT: Praeger, 2009); Robert Wistrich, *Holocaust Denial: The Politics of Perfidy* (Boston: De Gruyter, 2012). For instances of Genocide-Denial in other contexts, see (for Bosnia) Mark Danner, "American and the Bosnia Genocide," in *New York Review of Books* 44:19 (1997), Samantha Powers, "*A Problem from Hell*": *America and the Age of Genocide*, Ch 9 (New York: Basic Books, 2002); Ward Churchill, *A Little Matter of Genocide: Genocide and Denial in the Americas, 1492 to the Present* (San Francisco: City Lights, 1997); Lerna Ekmakcioglu, *Recovering Armenia: The Limits of Belonging in Post-Genocide Turkey* (Stanford: Stanford University Press, 2010); Stefan Ihrig, *Germany and the Armenians from Bismarck to Hitler* (Cambridge, MA: Harvard University Press, 2016); A. Dirk Moses, *Empire, Colony, Genocide: Conquest, Occupation, and Subaltern Resistance in World History* (New York: Berghahn Books, 2008).

On the conflict between Raphael Lemkin and Hersh Lauterpacht about the relative importance of genocide and human rights as such in UN legislation—between two central figures in the post–World War II legal and moral reaction to the war and its aftermath—see especially Ana Filipa Vrdoljak, "Human Rights and Genocide: The Work of Lauterpacht and Lemkin in Modern International Law," in *The European Journal of International Law* 20:4 (2010), and Philippe Sands, *East West Street: On the Origins of 'Genocide' and 'Crimes against Humanity'* (New York: Knopf, 2016).

Index

Index

Germany
  "Final Solution of the Jewish
    Question," 39, 58
  Nuremberg Laws, 24
  Nuremberg trials, 22,
    127–28
Goldwater, Barry, 149
Grotius, Hugo, 25, 111

Hausner, Gideon, 153
Hayes, Peter, 180
Himmler, Heinrich, 26, 28
Hitler, Adolf, 113
Hobbes, Thomas, 139
Holocaust, the
  Denial, 165–90
  "Final Solution of the Jewish
    Question," 28, 37–39, 58,
    116, 159–61, 171
  Linguistic analysis of term,
    114–17
  Uniqueness claim, 21, 118–20

International Court of Justice,
  23, 63
International Criminal Court,
  23, 61–62, 86, 103–6, 146,
  148, 193
Irving, David, 181–82
Israel, 111, 184, 189

Johnson, Lyndon, 149

Kant, Immanuel, 48, 51, 159
Karadzik, Radovan, 23
Kierkegaard, Søren, 149
Kovner, Abba, 124

Leibniz, Gottfried Wilhelm,
  37, 158

Lemkin, Raphael
  Biography, 110–13, 128–30
  Conceptualization of "geno-
    cide," 4–5, 21–26, 63, 88,
    95–96, 130–34, 142–43
Levi, Primo, 114, 160, 165
Lewis, Bernard, 66–68, 185
Lie, Trygve, 143
Lipstadt, Deborah, 181–82
Locke, John, 25
Luttwak, Edward, 145
Lyotard, Jean-Francois, 58

May, Larry, 64–66, 72–83, 87, 142
Mill, John Stuard, 188
Milton, John, 115
Mladic, Ratko, 23

Nichanian, Marc, 64–72

Plato, 37, 142, 157–58

Rights
  Group, 4, 29–32, 41–43, 74,
    91–98, 131–32, 137–48
  Natural, 25–26, 138–40, 142

Saint Paul, 158
Schabas, William, 102–5
Scholem, Gershom, 38, 151
Senesh, Hanna, 124
Shakespeare, William, 152–53
Soviet Union, 52, 57
Spinoza, Baruch, 37, 158
Stagneth, Bettina, 155–56

Thoreau, Henry David, 30

United Nations
  Convention on the Prevention

208

Index

Books by Berel Lang

Art and Inquiry
Philosophy and the Art of Writing
Act and Idea in the Nazi Genocide
The Anatomy of Philosophical Style
Writing and the Moral Self
Mind's Bodies: Thought in the Act
Heidegger's Silence
The Future of the Holocaust
Holocaust Representation: Art within the Limits of History and Ethics
Post-Holocaust: Interpretation, Misinterpretation, and the Claims of History
Philosophical Witnessing
Primo Levi: The Matter of a Life

Edited/Coedited Volumes

Marxism and Art: Writings in Aesthetics and Criticism
The Concept of Style
Philosophical Style
The Philosopher in the Community
The Death of Art
Writing and the Holocaust
Race and Racism in Theory and Practice
Method and Truth
The Holocaust: A Reader